What Readers Say

"Kevin has provided a powerful way to understand the principles and tools to help us become more inspiring leaders. It is a must read for anyone who wants to grow in their leadership skills. I find the Helm Model to be extremely effective."

—**David M. R. Covey**, coauthor of the bestselling book *Trap Tales: Outsmarting the 7 Hidden Obstacles to Success*

"If you read one book on leadership in the years ahead, make it this one. Kevin's practical approach to the things leaders do to take the helm is both inspiring and motivational. I have edited hundreds of books and articles on leadership and can unequivocally say this is one of the finest."

—**Ken Shelton**, author and founder of Executive Excellence

"We in Africa are excited to bring Kevin's powerful insights to our continent. We have long needed a clear, concise way to articulate leadership as we strive to take the helm of a rapidly changing world here in Ghana and all the other countries in Africa. The book is filled with practical ideas we all can start using immediately to become inspiring leaders in business, our homes, the community, and the world."

—**Mike Osikoya**, CEO of Mikensy Consulting in Ghana

"As you read this book and grasp the full power of the Helm Model, you will gain more skills and hope that you can become a more inspiring leader through the brilliant, simple, and everyday ideas Kevin is giving us. It's nice to read a book that gives power and hope to all of us in our important leadership roles."

—**Martin Hedley**, managing director, Vision Achievement Limited, United Kingdom

"I have known Kevin for 20 years and been part of his brilliant work. His insights into leadership and this very useful book and

Helm Module apply to all of us who want to become more effective leaders. I also recommend it for parents."

—**Bryan Inkley**, HR director, FireFly Equipment

"Leadership is crucial in healthcare as we navigate a changing future. The ideas and tools in Kevin's book help transform managers into inspiring leaders."

—**Beau Sorensen**, COO of First Choice Home Health and Hospice.

"For several decades, I have devoted myself to helping design instruction that enhances learning. Creative models are one great way to do this. Kevin's Helm Model does just that. Almost anyone can visually and mentally connect with the concept of a ship's helm and see how trust is the center axis. The five handles can be applied to any leadership challenge. I hope you will grasp the power of his model and follow his ideas on how to apply it in your own leadership and life challenges."

—**Max Cropper,** president and CEO of Five Star Performance Solutions

LEADERS DO FIVE THINGS

LEADERS DO FIVE THINGS

TAKING THE HELM IN A TURBULENT WORLD

KEVIN R. MILLER

Paperback ISBN 13: 978-1-4621-4846-2
eBook ISBN 13: 978-1-4621-4851-6

Published by Cedar Fort Publishing and Media

Library of Congress Cataloging Number: 2024939261

Cover design by Kent Miller

Illustrations by Izabela Ciesinska

Printed in the United States of America

10 9 8 7 6 5 4 3 2 1

Printed on acid-free paper

This book is dedicated to my wife and companion, Denise, for all she has taught me about excellence. As I have watched her in many leadership roles, I have seen constant excellence in action. I have enjoyed over four decades of traveling and learning adventures with her around the world. I also dedicate this book to my four children and six grandchildren.

It is also dedicated to the thousands of great leaders and parents who I have had the joy of meeting with and learning from these many years.

Special thanks to the following people for contributing their ideas to this book and the work of VisionBound: Denise Miller, Beau and Rachelle Sorensen, J. Lynn Jones, Kent Miller, Jason Miller, Christy Perry, Ben and Marianne Forstner, Bryan Inkley, Mike Osikoya, Fabrizio Ricciardi, and Enos Raharja.

Edited by Abigail Ellis and illustrated by Izabela Ciesinka.

Contents

Foreword

Five Alive: Keep Your Boat Afloat!
By Ken Shelton

Yes, my friends, this is yet another book on leadership—one of 10,000 books on leadership produced in the last 30 years, as Kevin R. Miller confesses upfront.

So, why buy it? Why read it? Why follow it? Because this one book captures the essence of the other 10,000! Believe me, I know. For 30 years, I served as editor/publisher of *Leadership Excellence* magazines and books. So, you can read the 10,000 books or the 6,000 articles we published by all the gurus, or you can read this one book and get the gist of it all.

As Henry David Thoreau said, "There are a thousand hacking at the branches of evil to one who is striking at the root." And I would paraphrase: For every 10,000 hacking at the leaves and branches of leadership, only one is striking at the root.

At the risk of hyperbole, I suggest Kevin is one striking at the root. He has a genius for *simplicity on the far side of complexity.*

Ship Metaphor for Leadership

I immediately identified with the ship metaphor. Both Kevin and I have spent many months of our lives on the water aboard a wide variety of vessels ranging from small one-man row boats to massive cruise ships and aircraft carriers, in Kevin's case. We have even "captained" a few ships of our own and learned that every leader is, in effect, captain of the ship. And job one is to keep the boat afloat,

the crew and passengers safe, and the ship ship-shape and seaworthy.

As you know, boats float when their weight is less than the weight of the water they displace. And ships (and their leaders) float or sink based on the same principle. In a poem, John Holmes tells of his boyhood experience with an old deaf New England shipbuilder who taught him without speaking: "As young Johnny watched the skilled hands of the old craftsman, it suddenly came to him with the force of a voice shouting in his ear: no matter how you build it, your ship must float. You can't explain to the ocean."

Likewise, Kevin intuits that one's leadership must float: you can't easily explain to an ocean of stakeholders why the ship is listing and sinking.

Whatever Makes Your Boat Float

While Kevin is prescriptive about his *five things,* he is less prescriptive about style. He's more into the expression "whatever floats your boat," meaning that you should do whatever makes you happy and successful and suits your personal taste, regardless of how others perceive it. It's an affirmation of individual preferences, implying that you should pursue what you like if it doesn't harm others. It's an acceptance of individuality and personal preference, essentially saying "you are entitled to your own preferences, even if others find them unusual or odd." It's an open-minded approach to the diverse ways people choose to live their lives or make decisions.

In this regard, Kevin reminds me of Joseph Smith Jr. When asked how he managed so many diverse people, he replied: "I teach them correct principles and they govern themselves."

This leadership style is counterintuitive to those who go by the dictum: "I preach to them current practices and programs and then govern by them."

Alas, many leader-ship captains fear giving people any discretionary time or freedom to make their own decisions. Perhaps they do this knowing what messes can be made. Tragically, many Titans have gone down with their Titanic to Davy Jones' locker, the oceanic abyss, the final resting place of drowned sailors and shipwrecked travelers, for failing to steer clear of icebergs and other dangerous obstacles. Hence, Miller advises those at the helm to beware of the barnacles and avoid "damn the torpedoes" recklessness, senseless onboarding and over-boarding, and difficult crewmembers and customers.

Since Kevin defines leadership as influence, his purpose is not "to further muddy the water" but instead "to present a simple visualization and analogy, along with practical tips and tools that can help each of unleash inspiring leadership at home or work or wherever the power of our influence is needed."

Again, he reminds us: "Our job as a leader is to have a firm but gentle hand on the helm. People look to us for strength and guidance and inspiration, and they want to trust both our character and competence. They want to feel confident and assured that our hand is on the helm."

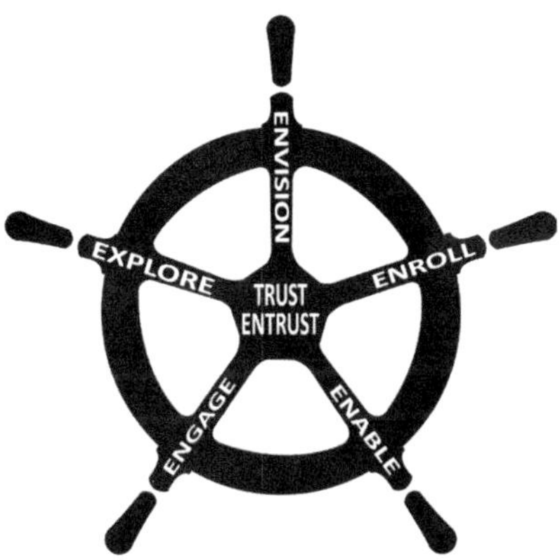

The helm of his ship has five major handles and a center axis, trust, which holds the helm in place and around which the other five actions—Envision, Enroll, Enable, Engage, and Explore—rotate. He also advocates rotational leadership: "A leader must be willing to let others, like the first mate, take the helm. Allow others to experience leadership and even to learn from mistakes. But be ready to step in and resume control or provide leadership and mentoring to keep the ship on track. The biggest danger of all may be personal egos. Never let egos get in the way of doing what is right for your team. When leaders allow their egos or self-serving agendas to override what needs to be done for the health and future of the organization the ship can easily crash into the rocks or become dead in the water."

He is convinced, as I am, that leaders and great leadership are the single greatest factor for unleashing the powerful potential in people and teams: "Leaders are truly force multipliers."

No Ship or Leadership Unsinkable

But he also warns us that no leader or ship is "unsinkable."

I agree. Once, I saw a production of ***The Unsinkable Molly Brown*** at the Hale Center Theater in Sandy, Utah. I came away thinking about how I see the same plot being played out before my eyes each day: proud captains sailing their big ships through berg-filled waters, thinking they are unsinkable, only to discover they are not. No Titan or Titanic is safe in today's waters.

United we stand, divided we fall; and pride always goes before the fall of all built on sand. And yet we still hear the call: Damn the torpedoes, full speed ahead . . . even though there are not enough life vests, lifeboats, and lifeguards to save us!

So, are we all destined to drown under poor leadership? No! Good golly, Miss Molly (or Mr. Miller) is here to save us from our folly, come Hale or high water!

—Ken Shelton

Ken Shelton served as founder of *Executive Excellence* and editor/publisher for 30 years. He is the author of *Beyond Counterfeit Leadership* and editor of dozens of other leadership books.

CHAPTER ONE

Introduction

Take the Helm!

Wait, not *another* book on *leadership*! If that's your thought, I don't blame you—over 10,000 books and even more articles and essays on leadership have been produced in just the past 30 years. Leadership has been the object of intense scrutiny almost since time began. The history of the world has been changed again and again because of a leader's influence, good or bad.

These names ring out to us across the centuries: Cyrus the Great, Pericles, Alexander the Great, George Washington, Jesus Christ, Nelson Mandela, Julius Caesar, Rameses II, Cleopatra VII, Qin Shi Huang, Charlemagne, Genghis Khan, Kwame Nkrumah, Mao Zedong, Mother Teresa, Queen Elizabeth I, Catherine the Great, Abraham Lincoln, Tecumseh, Napoleon Bonaparte, and even Adolf Hitler, to name a few.

You might question my judgement or even my sanity in listing some of these names together. Jesus Christ, George Washington, and Nelson Mandela listed with Adolf Hitler and Mao Zedong? When we define leadership as *influence*, as we will later, the reasoning becomes clear. Ultimately, that is what leadership is all about. Every one of those individuals exerted great influence that is even felt today.

My purpose in writing this book is to not further muddy the water, but instead to present a simple visualization and analogy, along with practical tips and tools that can help unleash inspiring leadership at home or work or wherever the power of our influence is needed. Leaders, in great measure, shape the culture of the organizations they lead, both micro and macro (see Chapter Three).

Perhaps this quote by Winston Churchill sets the stage for what this book is about:

> To every man there comes in his lifetime that special moment when he is figuratively tapped on the shoulder and offered a chance to do a very special thing, unique to him and fitted to his talents. What a tragedy if that moment finds him unprepared or unqualified for that which would be his finest hour.

Of course, this quote equally applies to women, but the point is clear: we need to be prepared to lead in the challenging times ahead. These can become our "finest hours." My intent is that this book will provide ideas on how to prepare for these challenges.

Let's not proceed without a simple definition of leadership. Plato said, "The beginning of wisdom is the definition of terms." I have read numerous definitions of leadership, but for simplicity's sake, let's start with this: *Leadership is the art of influencing others toward accomplishing mutual objectives.*

I will address how this differs from management later in the book (and leadership is much different than management).

I will not try to promote any style of leadership: all those listed leaders had different styles and so will you. Chapter Four addresses the most common styles.

I will structure this book around the analogy of a ship, perhaps a "leader-ship," and the critical role of leaders in taking the helm. I like stories, especially ones that illustrate key principles. So, this story below will help illustrate the power of leadership and later the Helm Model that will follow.

Years ago, I was working with a police department. It had suffered for over twenty years under the iron hand of an authoritative police chief. He was not a bad man, but his approach to leadership was "catch everyone and anyone doing wrong" and humiliate them accordingly. One of his favorite tactics and tools was to "write up" an officer or staff member for any infraction and file these notices or warnings in a special file cabinet in his office. The file was his "pride and joy," and an ongoing record of his dealings with his team. It was so bad that officers and staff would do anything to avoid him. One man told me that once the closest door to him when the chief was coming was the lady's restroom. He stepped in and said, "Chief is coming," and they understood! You can well imagine that this leader's behavior created a terrible work culture.

Finally, it was time for the chief to retire, and a new police chief was hired, a man who had an entirely different approach to leadership. He quickly realized that he was about to take the helm of a very dysfunctional department. Morale was in the tank. Trust in leadership was almost non-existent. Individual and team performance was at a low.

In his first meeting with the outgoing chief, the new chief was shown the "special file cabinet," and the outgoing chief told him to read all the files and he would know everything he needed to know about the department. The new chief just nodded and thanked him. This single act by the outgoing leader showed the new chief what the main problem was.

The next day was the first time for him to meet all the rather expectant but nervous officers and staff. The chairs were arranged in semi circles as they walked in and there, in the middle, stood the hated file cabinet. They all knew what it was, and they looked at each other with horror, wondering what was in store. Precisely on time, the new chief walked in dressed to the nines in a sharp uniform.

He then demonstrated one of the most powerful leadership moments imaginable. He smiled and welcomed everyone to the meeting. He walked over and laid his hand on the file cabinet and said, "I know all of you know what is in this cabinet. I give you my word as an officer and a gentleman that I have not opened or read any of the material or files in this cabinet, and I never will. I will prove it to you."

With that, he motioned his hand and his secretary pushed in an industrial grade shredder on a pushcart. He turned it on and began shredding the files one at a time. Tears welled up in eyes around the room. He then simply said, "As of this moment each one of you is the finest law enforcement officer in the country. Continue to show that to me. I will meet each one of you personally later in the week. Dismissed." And he walked out.

The officers and staff sat a moment in silence, absorbing what had just taken place. At that moment one of the senior officers looked around with tears in his eyes and said, "We will *never* let that man down. Understood?"

As time went on, they didn't. The new chief earned, in one short meeting, a level of trust and commitment that no nasty file cabinet ever could. In essence, he reset the culture. Yet, as time went on, the overall performance of the entire team was greater than ever.

I believe you can get the gist and the power of this example. It did not take the new chief months to right the ship. He largely did it in one ten-minute meeting. Such is the power of creative, inspired leadership in resetting the culture.

Introducing the Helm Model

Please consider your organization as if it is a ship sailing along in sometimes calm, but often turbulent waters. The ship is your *organization*, whether a family, a team, or a large company. The crew of the ship is your *staff* or others whose everyday actions affect the functioning of the ship and influence its culture. The passengers of the ship are your customers, clients, vendors, or members who choose to join you in your journey for a purpose.

That central purpose should be the basis of your mission and your vision and your values and how you measure success. It serves as your North Star, which we will address in Chapter Five. The ship's itinerary is your strategic plan and goals and how you execute the vision and mission.

Ideally, but rarely, your ship sails smoothly along, successfully hitting each goal and arriving at each port until it achieves your main goals. But storms arise that can blow your ship off target or cause you to reroute. An unexpected example is the COVID storm.

The *culture* of your ship and team affects the behavior of your crew and sometimes even leads to outright mutiny like what happened on the HMS Bounty in 1789.

The poor, dictatorial leadership of the outgoing police chief shows how poor leadership guts the morale, performance, and motivation of a team.

Our job as a leader is to have a firm but gentle hand on the helm. People look to us for strength and guidance and inspiration, and they want to trust both our character and competence. *They want to feel confident and assured that our hand is on the helm.*

The model is illustrated in the model picture above. The helm of the ship has five major handles and a center axis, trust, which holds the helm in place and around which the other five actions rotate.

Let me briefly explain the Helm Model and then go in more depth in successive chapters.

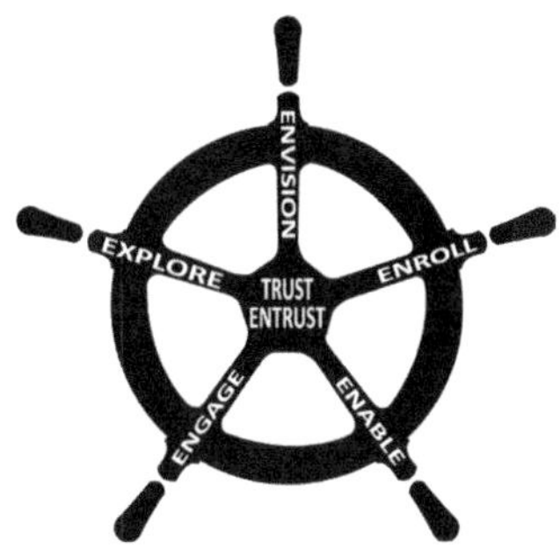

The first and perhaps the most important role is to **Envision**. A leader guides the organization in creating a very clear vision, mission, values, and measures of success, all driven through a consequential strategic plan. This becomes the North Star. All further actions and decisions must be made in alignment with this overarching and inspiring purpose. We will address the process of creating this North Star in Chapter Five.

Once we have this vision clearly in place, we must then **Enroll** people. Each of our crew members is made up of four dimensions: physical, mental, emotional, and spiritual components. Each one

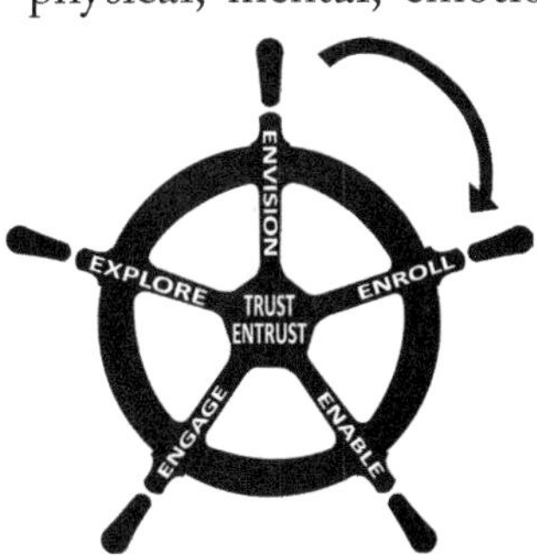

of these can and must be enrolled and inspired in the vision. *Yet statistics show that only about 15% of people can accurately and clearly identify the mission, vision, strategy, and goals of the organization they are working in!* They simply have not been enrolled by their leaders. In such a situation, work can become a sort of "day prison," where people are admitted at eight and released at five. We will address this in Chapter Six.

But now imagine that you and your people have a clear vision and are enrolled in it. Now everyone must be **Enabled**. In fact, it is very frustrating for people to feel excited by the vision and to be enrolled in it but are then disabled by the lack of resources, authority, training, or a myriad of other things which they need to carry out the vision and strategy. *In fact, I would prefer not to be enrolled at all than to be enrolled and then disabled.* Jack Welch reportedly said, "If you try to motivate people without training them, you only frustrate them." This is also true with the other things that people need to be enabled. This is addressed in Chapter Seven.

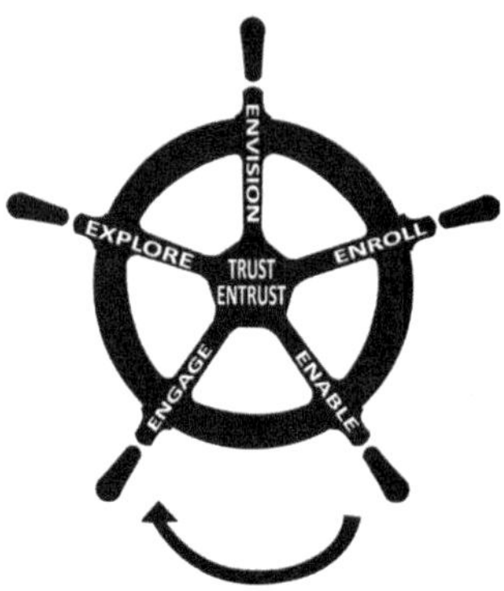

Once people have the vision and are enrolled in it and are mostly or fully enabled, we can now **Engage** them. It is difficult to engage people who lack the first three elements. But I have found that if the first three are firmly in place very little needs to be done to engage them. They will actively and creatively figure things out and self-release their own potential. We will address this in Chapter Eight.

Finally, we need everyone in the organization to actively and continuously **Explore** new and better ways to carry out the vision and strategy. Exploring does not belong only to the role of senior leaders and managers. In fact, another study suggests that over 60% of the ideas that truly revolutionize organizations come from people who have only been there less than a year! They have not been there long

enough to become part of the scenery. They see things in fresh eyes. Remember that no matter how well our organization is going, if we are not continually exploring new horizons and new ways to do business or create new products, we may find our ship dead in the water or torpedoed by your competition! See Chapter Nine for ideas on creating an exploring culture focused on learning and improving.

But finally, what must we have at the center core of the wheel to tightly join the five leadership components together? That axis is **trust**. In fact, this trust axis may be the most important part of the assembly. In our analogy, trust is that axis. Stephen M. R. Covey, in his book *The Speed of Trust*, writes that trust is the "one thing that changes everything." Trust exists in both the people and the systems. In high trust systems, everything moves faster and cheaper as Covey points out. A well lubricated axis that is constantly monitored and maintained enables the helm to move smoothly and effectively. But if it is allowed to get rusty and unable to freely turn, there inevitably will be negative results. We will address trust in Chapter Ten.

There will be times that our organization needs a powerful and steady and decisive hand on the helm, especially during times of change and turmoil. And few other times in modern history have presented a world-wide pandemic challenge like COVID-19. Such a steady hand of leadership inspires confidence. Other times things are going well and only a light finger on the helm is needed to make tweaks and adjustments. Also, a leader must be willing to let others, like the first mate, take the helm. Allow others to experience leadership and even to learn from mistakes. But be ready to step in and resume control or provide leadership and mentoring to keep the ship on track.

We see many of the elements in the Helm Model in the previous story of the incoming police chief. First, he had a vision of what this department could be—the finest law enforcement team in the nation. He needed to quickly enroll the team in the vision. He saw that trust, the center hub, was practically non-existent. He did not need a long speech. He just needed to earn trust and, in essence, "hit the reset button." He did it in one ten-minute meeting.

The remaining chapters in the book will enhance this Helm Model. In Chapter Eleven, I address several "barnacles" that can build up on the hull of your ship and slow its progress and even sink it. In Chapter Twelve, I will address other dangers that can also symbolically sink your ship.

Since all organizations are somehow involved in serving others, Chapter Thirteen addresses how we create loyalty through a service-centric culture. And to conclude I will illustrate in Chapter Fourteen how the power of love is crucial to leadership.

Let us now sail forward exploring these chapters and explore each one of these after first defining the importance of culture and the power of leadership.

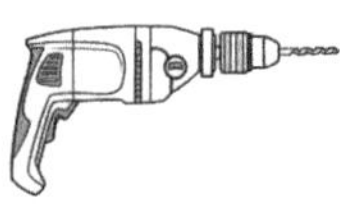

Watch for this Power Tool Icon along the way! In various pages of this book, you will find this icon. It signals one powerful tip or idea you can use to become a more effective leader.

This idea icon will signify a particularly important concept or idea.

My intention with this book is to underscore the incredible power of leadership and provide the principles and tools to help anyone become a more effective leader. I will let the ship analogy unfold largely by itself through your own observations and experience.

The toolbox sections at the end will provide further ideas that build on the model.

Let us now sail on and define the importance of culture and the power of leadership before exploring the rest of the chapters.

CHAPTER TWO

Leadership

The Force Multiplier

"Leadership is the greatest force multiplier on the battlefield."

When I was a young Army lieutenant in Germany over forty years ago, we were "in the field" learning how to lead soldiers in combat. Our trainer that day was a seasoned Green Beret Master Sergeant who had fought in places nearly the world over and had battle scars to prove it. We were fumbling around trying to effectively lead our squads and platoons, and he became increasingly frustrated and brought us together in a circle. He threw his helmet on the ground and said something I have never forgotten. "Leadership is the greatest force multiplier on the battlefield, and I am not seeing s - - t."

I remember dutifully writing down that statement in the little green pocket field book we always carried. I did not fully understand what he meant those many years ago, but now I believe it and have seen and proven it over and over in the decades since.

A force multiplier is anything added to a force or system that multiplies its power or effectiveness. After over thirty years of developing military, corporate, and academic leaders, I am now more convinced of his words than ever. *Not only is leadership a "force multiplier," it is* ***THE*** *greatest force multiplier that can be applied to any organization or system.*

This is historically obvious on the battlefields of war. Since the quote has a "battlefield" connotation, let me illustrate it with some military examples. Similar examples would abound in business, education, healthcare, government, and other human endeavors.

The leadership of Robert E. Lee and Thomas "Stonewall" Jackson was a force multiplier for an undermanned, inexperienced, and under-equipped Confederate army in the first eighteen months of the American Civil War. Time and again, these Confederate leaders out thought and out maneuvered their Union counterparts. Regardless of the debatable cause of the Confederacy, the brilliance and personal courage of much of their battlefield leadership is not in question. "Stonewall" Jackson got his name during the gunfire and confusion of the Battle of Bull Run. Another Confederate general, Barnard E. Bee rallied his troops by saying, "There is Jackson, standing like a stone wall." If the Union army had been blessed with this caliber of leaders, the war would have likely ended in under a year.

George Washington, "Blackjack" Pershing, George S. Patton, Napoleon, Cyrus the Great, Alexander the Great—all were force multipliers on the battlefield. The names of great military leaders ring out through history, and there are many lists of great leaders found online. It is equally true in other settings.

Think about how these leaders led their organizations through challenging times with firm hands on the helm and how they were personally inspiring and motivating in different ways. Think of the force multipliers you have known in your life: perhaps a teacher, coach, parent, family member, or even a neighbor.

For this reason, Robert Frost said, "I am more afraid of an army of sheep led by a lion than an army of lions led by a sheep."

However, in a very real sense, we are all engaged on battlefields of our own as we tackle the tests of leading ourselves, our families, and our service organizations against a formidable array of challenges.

Every organization has within it great potential force. This force is constituted by almost everything within the organization, from its people to its systems, products, and services. This force has potent and almost always untapped potential.

I believe that leaders, and great leadership, are the single greatest factor for unleashing this potential force.

Leaders are truly force multipliers. Unfortunately, poor leadership is a force de-multiplier. I have seen inspiring leaders change the culture and begin multiplying the force almost immediately upon their arrival. I have seen the opposite as well.

John Buchan said, "The task of leadership is not to put greatness into people, but to elicit it. The greatness is already there." We must believe this: people are the greatest resource on the earth, and unlimited potential lies within every person. Leaders have the opportunity and the challenge of releasing, aligning, and focusing this potential.

The same thing applies in all situations from business and nonprofit organizations to religious and school systems. *When you inject inspirational leadership into the force, it multiplies virtually everything.*

Warren Bennis said, "Leadership.... That's it. Give me, for example, a rotten school system, a decrepit schoolhouse, a school budget crisis but a great principal, and you've got a good-to-great school. Give me great systems, great facility, etc., but a rotten principal and you've got a poor-to-awful school." One could replace the educational example in his quote with virtually any other human endeavor, and it would be equally true.

Dr. Peter F. Drucker was a profound thought leader about leadership. He made the astute observation, "Only three things happen naturally in organizations: friction, confusion, and underperformance. Everything else requires leadership."

I often use this quote in my leadership courses and ask, "Why is the natural state of human beings to move toward friction, confusion, and underperformance without leadership?" The answers are varied, but most people understand that even the very best, most motivated individuals will naturally begin gravitating toward their view of how things should be done, resulting in friction and confusion that eventually can lead to underperformance. Leaders provide the force multiplier vision and power that overcomes this. *A thoughtful correlation might be that whenever you see any signs of friction, confusion, and underperformance, it could be due to a lack of leadership.*

As a leader, we are like the thermostat on the wall of a room. In great measure, we set the tone or "temperature" of the organization. If we are enthused and passionate, the people will likely be that as well. If we are negative and dispassionate, we "chill" the organization. *It is an almost immeasurable power and responsibility.*

Great leaders arise during times of great challenge. Had there not been a Second World War, there would not have been the greatness of Dwight D. Eisenhower. If there had been no issues with apartheid, there may have been no Nelson Mandela. No civic suffering, no Mother Teresa. To be a great leader, we must expect times of challenge.

A very recent example is the inspiring leadership of Volodymyr Zelenskyy of Ukraine. His courage under fire and ability to unite his people have been an inspiration to millions. You may know that soon after the Russian invasion one country offered Zelenskyy a free airplane extraction out of his country. His brilliant retort was, "I need ammunition, not a ride." He courageously stood in front of his country, on camera, inspiring them with his vision and determination.

John Foster Dulles said, "The sign of a successful organization is not whether you have significant problems to deal with, but whether they are the same problems you were dealing with last year." There will *never* be a time when your team, family, organization, or nation will not have significant problems to deal with. Successful and well-led organizations grow beyond their problems, solve them, and face new ones every year. I recently saw a man in the Boston airport wearing a T-shirt with a quote from Nelson Mandela: *"I never lose. I either win, or I learn."*

Centuries ago, Plato said, "The beginning of wisdom is the definition of terms." Whole essays and books have been written defining leadership but let me add a few definitions here just to set the stage for what we will address in the rest of the book.

At the beginning of this book, I offered this basic definition of leadership: "Leadership is the art of influencing others toward accomplishing a mutual objective." The keywords are *influencing* and *mutual objective*. Notice this definition implies nothing evil or good: it could apply to Adolf Hitler or Jesus Christ. It implies that leadership is an *art*, while management is more of a *science*.

In their superb book, *The Leadership Challenge*, Kouzes and Posner defined leadership as "the art of mobilizing and inspiring others to *want* to struggle for shared aspirations."

A statement by President and General Dwight D. Eisenhower reflects this idea: "Leadership is getting someone to do something you want them to do because they want to do it!"

Dr. Stephen R. Covey once said, "Leadership is the creation of a culture or relationship surrounding a common vision." He later added, "Leadership is communicating to another person their worth and potential so clearly that they come to see it in themselves."

John Quincy Adams defined it this way: "If your actions inspire others to dream more, learn more, do more and become more, you are a leader."

Another of my personal favorites is the U.S. Army definition: *"Leadership is the process of influencing people by providing purpose, direction, and motivation to accomplish the mission and improve the organization."* I like this because of the two-fold outcome: accomplish the mission *and* improve the organization.

We probably have seen leaders focus on accomplishing a mission but leave the organization and relationships in shambles; in essence, killing the goose to get the golden eggs.

Note that in all these definitions, there are several themes: emphasizing personal influence rather than relying on the use of power; focusing on a mutual purpose or vision; igniting the worth and potential of others; and providing purpose, motivation, and direction.

If you pause to think about the greatest influencers or leaders in your life, you will likely see them exemplifying the definitions above.

Leadership Differs from Management

A simple definition of management might be "planning, organizing, directing, controlling and evaluating the processes and resources of an organization."

Warren Bennis and Burt Nanus wrote the following in their book *Leadership: The Strategies for Taking Charge:* "To manage means to bring about, accomplish, to have charge or responsibility for, to conduct. Leading is influencing, guiding in direction, course, action, opinion. The distinction is crucial. Managers are people who do things right, and leaders are people who do the right thing."

I once heard it put simply: *"Management is power **over** people. Leadership is power **with** people."*

Therefore, management is typically *positional.* It is derived by a position on an organization chart. Leadership is not necessarily positional. It is attained, won, and maintained by personal actions, character, and the ability to influence. That is why some of the greatest and most inspirational leaders are not found on an organization chart and may be scattered through every level of a team or organization.

My friend and mentor, Stephen R. Covey, made the astute observation that "most organizations are overmanaged and underled."

Perhaps that is why Admiral Thomas Moorer said, "There is a difference between leadership and management. Leadership is of the spirit, compounded of personality, vision, and training. Its practice is an art. Management is a science of the mind. Managers are necessary; leaders are indispensable."

We are heading into times of unprecedented change in the world, and as said by Warren Bennis, "In times of rapid change, there is no substitute for leadership."

Dr. Covey raised a challenge: "The call and need of a new era is for greatness. Tapping into the higher reaches of human genius and motivation requires leaders to have a new mindset, a new skill set, and a new toolset."

The Little Things Are often the Biggest Things

In leadership, the little things are often the biggest things in showing your people they matter and creating loyalty. Leadership releases human potential. I will illustrate the Helm Model with two more examples:

I was serving as a company commander in the 7th Infantry Division at Fort Ord, California, when a friend told me an amazing story relayed to him by his brother. His brother was the personal pilot for General Norman Schwarzkopf, the I Corps Commander "Stormin' Norman," who later commanded Operation Desert Storm. The pilot was critical for the general, whose life was literally in his hands.

One day, the general climbed into his seat as they were about to take off for an important meeting about an hour away from the post. The pilot asked the general what time the meeting was likely to end. The general told him about 15:00. He could see that was good news for the pilot. The general said, "That seems to be important to you. Tell me why."

The pilot tried to brush it off, but the general insisted. The pilot told him it was his little girl's fourth birthday, and a party was scheduled for 16:00. She asked him if he could come, and he said he would try. Well, the meeting dragged on (the two biggest problems in America are making ends meet and meetings end).

The pilot's sole role was to sit quietly and wait for the meeting to end. Suddenly, General Schwarzkopf jumped to his feet, told the next senior leader in the room to take over the meeting, and rushed out the door. The pilot chased him to the helicopter and in surprise asked, "Where are we going, sir?"

The general said, "Get this bird in the air, we have a birthday party to get to!"

The pilot's quarters were a distance from the airfield and the general saw they would not make it to the party by 16:00 if they landed at the airfield. So, the general got on the radio, called the military police, and told them to set up a landing zone in the post chapel's parking lot not far from the pilot's quarters. (The pilot later told his brother he didn't even know the general knew where he lived!)

With the general leading the way, they rushed to the quarters and burst in the door at exactly 16:00. The little girl rushed to her daddy and said, "I didn't think you could come."

General Schwarzkopf picked the little girl up and said, "Do you think we would miss *your* party, sweetheart?"

They stayed for the party and played games with the children. The pilot saw the three-star general on his knees playing Barbie with the little girls. The pilot said he stood in the door with tears in his eyes. Later, he told his brother, "I would fly to hell and back for Norman Schwarzkopf."

This is an incredible example that illustrates much of the Helm Model, especially enrolling and engaging. First, the general knew where his pilot lived and knew there was a chapel nearby. Second, the general paid attention to the details and knew how important that party was to his pilot. It has been wisely said that "what is important to another person should be as important to you as the other person is to you." So, the little girl's party was as important to the general as his pilot was. This single act of love from a leader made a huge deposit in the emotional bank account of that pilot, who undoubtedly shared it far and wide.

I read another example in a story called "Jessie's Glove" in the outstanding book, *Heart at Work*. The story's author, Rick Phillips, was leading a discussion with a group of managers for Circle K, a convenience store, and asked, "What has caused you stay long enough in the company to become a manager?" One woman said, "It was the cost of a Little League Baseball glove."

The woman was a single mother who had only been working there a short time. She had taken the job only as an interim step. While at work, she fielded a phone call from her young son, Jessie. She had to explain to him that money was tight and that he would have to wait for the baseball glove he needed.

The next morning, Patricia, the store manager, called the woman into her office. The woman was confused and worried if she had done something wrong. Patricia said, "I overheard you talking to your son yesterday and I know how hard it is to explain things to kids. This is a baseball glove for Jessie because he may not understand how important he is to you even though you must pay bills before you can buy gloves. You know we can't pay good people like you as much as we would like to. But we do care and I want you to know you are important to us."

Patricia communicated value to this woman by enrolling her and engaging her. And enabling her to help her son play baseball! The little things are the big things. This act won so much loyalty that the woman went on to become a store manager herself and shared this story in a management meeting. (Imagine how she likely treats her staff in return!)

The author of the story, Rick Phillips, ends by writing that this story vividly demonstrates that people often remember more about how an employer *cares* than what an employer *pays*: "An important lesson for the price of a Little League Baseball glove."

In conclusion, I return to the premise of this chapter: "Leadership is the greatest force multiplier."

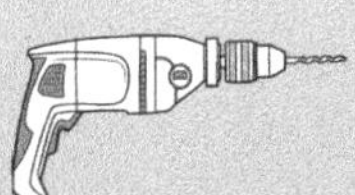

Tool Time: Listen with your eyes, ears, and heart. Pay attention to the details around you and tune yourself to hear those little things that can make such a difference to those you lead, including your family members.

"If you want to go fast, go alone. If you want to go far, go together." —African Proverb

---

CHAPTER THREE

Leaders Change the Culture!

Super Bowl 54 was played on February 2, 2020, and was watched by over 100 million people. It was an exciting game between the Kansas City Chiefs and the San Francisco 49ers. My wife and I were torn in our allegiance to a team. I was raised in California, and we later lived there in the Army. But our hearts ended up supporting the Kansas City Chiefs because we were also stationed near there at Fort Leavenworth with the Army.

There were a lot of celebrations on the field and at home after the Chiefs won. To me, one of the most significant remarks came from one of the prominent sports commentators. As we watched the Chiefs celebrate and the joyous reaction of the Chief's head coach, Andy Reid, the commentator emphasized the power of leadership which Coach Reid brought to the team. The commentator gave a tribute that I have never forgotten: *"Coach Reid started changing the culture the moment he walked in the locker room."*

The power of Coach Reid's leadership was evident in the faces of his players as they rushed to hug their coach and pour ice cold Gatorade over his head. The commentator went on to say, "The coach loves his players, and they love him." Of course, love was not enough for them to win the game and the season. It took the skill of a superb coach who kept a steady hand at the helm. But his love for his players did much to win their loyalty and release their full power on the field.

When one of my close associates, John Norton, was working on his master's degree in organizational behavior (MAOB) at Brigham Young University, one of the first things they focused on was learning how to assess the culture of an organization. The simple definition for culture they learned was that "culture is the way things are done around here." To better understand it as student teams, they selected businesses to observe how people interacted and spoke with each other. Special attention was paid to how leadership and management engaged their members and how the organization reacted to their influence. It was clear that much of the culture was driven by the personality, behavior, and leadership style of the leader.

The lesson here is clear to all of us who aspire to great leadership. As a leader, we influence the culture every time we walk in the room. It radiates in almost every word we say and write. It oozes out of the memos and how we conduct meetings. It is charged in the way we encourage, coach, and counsel, and how we listen to, respect, and learn from others. Cultures are influenced in nearly every policy we make.

Before we make any decision or make any change we must stop and ask ourselves, *"Will this have a positive or a negative effect on the culture of this organization?"* I find this question is asked far too rarely because so many decisions are made based merely upon a monetary bottom line.

Many years ago, the late great Dr. Peter F. Drucker made a powerful statement: "Culture eats strategy for breakfast." I am sure it was the impetus for *Culture Eats Strategy for Lunch*, a best-selling business book written years later by Curt Coffman.

No matter how fancy and sophisticated our vision and mission and strategy is, our culture will eat it for breakfast and either make it fail or succeed. In my consulting, I have come to see that the best strategies will fail in a bad culture. On the other hand, a less than perfect strategy can brilliantly succeed in a high trust, energized culture.

Culture penetrates everything. It either *zaps* or *saps* the energy of people and systems.

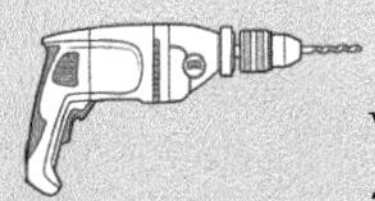

Tool Time: Better or Different? Years ago, I was given advice from a close relative who told me a hint about parenting: "If you want someone to do better, never make them feel worse." I tried to follow her advice in my parenting, but confess it is not easy.

To some degree this same idea can apply in many or most situations. There are obviously times when we need to give counsel or correct things, but the way we do it can build or hurt relationships and the trust they are built on. It can come down to the words we use. Instead of saying "Here's something you can do better," say "I have an idea on how you can do that differently." There is a world of difference between the word "better" and the word "differently." Better implies something is negative or even bad. Different just suggests a more effective way. Try it!

If we step back and look at organizational culture, we can really see that it is a composite of personal and individual cultures. Each one of us has a personal culture. We radiate that culture by our words and actions to those around us. Because of leaders' all-important role in the organization, they must be particularly aware of their own personal cultures and what they are radiating to those around them. Bringing all these individual cultures together and aligning them in the further systems' culture results in the overall culture of the organization.

Ultimately, a major premise of my book is about what we as leaders need to do and must do to transform the culture of an organization. In a great measure, leaders are dealers in hope: through personal action and example. President Barak Obama said, "The best way to not feel hopeless is to get up and do something. Don't wait for good things to happen to you. If you go out and make some good things happen, you will fill the world with hope, you will fill yourself with hope."

Key Points: As a leader, pay close attention to your own personal culture. Periodically, ask yourself, "Would I like working for me?" (Perhaps stand in front of a mirror when you ask it.) Am I an energizer or de-energizer? Do I radiate a positive, we-can-do-it spirit?

Don't Forget to Sharpen the Saw

It is difficult to maintain the self-control and focus needed to be an energizing, positive culture leader if we are not first talking care of ourselves. Christ Himself said, "Love thy neighbor as thyself" (Matthew 22:38). Self-love and self-care are essential to our ability to think clearly and be effective culture leaders.

Abraham Lincoln reportedly said, "If I had six hours to cut down a tree, I would spend four of them sharpening my axe." It is easy, as leaders, to symbolically keep piling up the wood in front of ourselves and our staff, requiring more and more and setting higher and higher goals. This creates a fear-based, impossible-to-succeed culture that deflates individuals and teams.

Each of us are made up of at least four major dimensions: physical, mental, emotional, and spiritual. Each of these dimensions is like a saw that needs constant nourishment and sharpening.

This relates to the Whole Person Paradigm, taught by Dr. Stephen R. Covey in his writings and programs. His concept is that each of us is a person with four elements: physical, mental, emotional, and spiritual. These align with the body, mind, heart, and spirit.

For the mind, Covey outlines the need to **clarify purpose**. This aligns with my thoughts in Chapter Five on the importance of creating a North Star vision and mission. Next, what do people need for the body and heart to be fully released? In his model, **aligning systems** helps accomplish this. Covey also details that **unleashing talent** happens when we align systems and engage people. This aligns with the Helm Model of Enrolling and Engaging. Chapters Six and Seven offer further ideas.

Covey taught that the center of his model, spirit, is released when we **inspire trust**. I put it in the center of my Helm Model and address it further in Chapter Ten.

Aesop's famous tale of the Goose and the Golden Egg reminds us of what happens when we kill the goose to get the golden eggs. Only then do we find out we have killed the very source of the treasure and can get no more. To not kill the goose, great leaders take care of themselves physically, through exercise, nutrition, hydration, rest, and stress management. They encourage staff to do so as well and bring elements of fun and stress management to the workplace.

I have known clients who bring in office masseurs to give free massages, set up nap rooms where staff can sign out for a power nap, and do a myriad of other things to make work relaxing and empowering. They almost universally report results in higher productivity, greater creativity, and higher retention.

As an Army officer, I experienced a situation in Fort Ord, California, where the commanding general of the 7th Infantry Division directed and enforced that people to go home no later than six at night and he set the example. He sent the military police out to see which cars were still in the parking lots and where the office lights were on. (Of course, it could not apply everywhere: hospitals and police must stay operational 24/7 and often combat units were deployed on field exercises.) But his point was clear: *being busy and working long hours does not necessarily equate to effective productivity.*

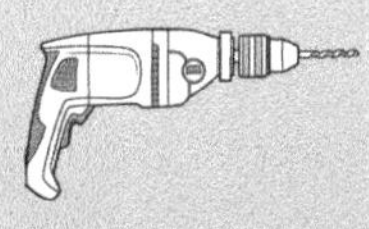

Application Ideas

1. Think about your personal culture and how it might be affecting others. If you would like to participate in a strength-based 360-degree personal profile you can gather input from all those around you on how you are influencing them, the team and the culture. Contact us at VisionBound to learn more.

2. Free Culture Survey Offer!

It is important to diagnose before prescribing. We have created a powerful online survey you can use to gauge the current culture of your organization. We can set this survey up for you and customize it to your organization. You send it out to all your staff, and we will tabulate and analyze the results and present them back to you at no cost nor further obligation. Contact us at www.VisionBound.com to see a sample of the report and how we can customize it.

So, let's continue to unravel how leaders create this culture by going through all the six elements in our Helm Model. However, before we begin, consider what your leadership style is.

The next chapter will introduce the styles of leaders. This will help you be able to determine which is your predominant style and how will you use it in guiding your "leader-ship."

CHAPTER FOUR

So, What is Your Leadership Style?

The great Nelson Mandela said something very apt about leadership. He said, "A leader is like a shepherd. He stays behind the flock, letting the nimblest go out ahead, whereupon the others follow, not realizing that all along that they are being directed from behind."

Leaders use many different styles to release their influence. Some are flamboyant, like General George S. Patton, with his ivory-handled revolvers, standing on top of a tank in a jammed intersection directing traffic himself in the Battle of the Bulge. Others demonstrate a quiet, almost under-the-surface leadership, like Mother Teresa. General George Marshall, whose Marshall Plan enabled the post-war recovery of the former enemies of Japan and Germany, was known for his clear, non-flamboyant style. Nelson Mandela is one of the greatest and most influential people of the last century. He led with a calm and even quiet style.

Lao Tzu said it best regarding this style: "A leader is best when people barely know he exists, when his work is done, his aim fulfilled, they will say: we did it ourselves."

We can each choose our own style, but the outcome will be the same: We are either multiplying the force or sucking the potential out of it with almost every word, action, and policy we generate.

Types of Leadership Styles

Much has been written about the styles of leadership. Over time, leaders develop their own style of leadership shaped by many factors, including personality, upbringing, experience, and the maturity, needs, and culture of the team or organization they are leading. Plus, events themselves shape leaders. Had there not been apartheid, there might not have been a Nelson Mandela. Without World War II, Dwight D. Eisenhower would hardly be a footnote in history. This will likely be true for you.

Here are seven common styles of leadership—which one fits you? Which styles, or combination of styles, have you used, or a combination of them?

However, before we begin, I have one important caveat. Leadership styles, like personality styles, have many deep roots. We may come onto the earth with a disposition or inclination towards a certain style, as I have noticed in my own four children. But we also have a myriad of other influences from our experiences, our environment, and even what we eat and drink. Our styles may evolve over time and certainly by the situations we face. So, in the following sections, I am not being prescriptive, only instructive.

Whichever style we use as leaders, all of us can be "Trim Tabs." Along the outer edge of the massive, multistory rudder of a large ocean liner, there is a slim trim tab. When the steering wheel moves the trim tab, it creates just enough suction to move the larger rudder. This observation applies to leadership and was first used by the designer, Buckminster Fuller. In February 1972, Fuller said: "Something hit me very hard once, thinking about what one little man could do. Think of the Queen Mary—there's a tiny thing at the edge of the rudder called a trim tab. It's a miniature rudder. Just moving the little trim tab builds a low pressure that pulls the rudder around. It takes almost no effort at all. I realized: One little individual can be a trim tab. If you're doing dynamic things mentally, you can just put your foot out and direct where the whole big ship of state is going to go."

In February 1984, Stephen R. Covey and Ken Shelton applied the trim tab metaphor to personal and team leadership in writing *The Seven Habits of Highly Effective People*. This definition is found in their book:

> A *trim-tab leader* is one who is not necessarily a leader by position but by choice—one who can directly or indirectly affect change within and without his circle of influence by being proactive or by taking initiative. Trim-tab leaders apply vision, discipline, passion and conscience to the outside edge of their circle of influence, thus causing it to expand.

Ken Shelton cited another recent example. In 2019 actor Jeff Bridges used Fuller's metaphor in his Cecil B. DeMille Award acceptance speech at the 76th Golden Globes: "Bucky made the analogy that a trim tab is an example of how one individual can affect society. I like to think of myself as a trim tab. All of us are trim tabs. We might think we're not up to the task, but we are. We're alive! We can make a difference! We can turn this ship in the way we want to go!"

1. Autocratic Leadership Style

This is a strong one-dimensional leadership style that grants almost full power or authority to the leader, boss, or manager. Leaders typically "call the shots" and make most decisions without much or any consultation with others. Autocratic leaders communicate expectations to team members and expect them to act on them immediately. This style can be effective in certain situations, especially in emergencies or when a leader inherits a very broken, disorganized, dysfunctional team that is desperate for a firm hand on the wheel. Keep in mind that this style can get quick results rather soon, but its effectiveness wears off over time. Autocratic leaders, even autocratic parents, find they must keep increasing their autocracy to get the same or better results. Soon, people resent this style of leadership and consciously or subconsciously begin to rebel.

A terrible example of this came to me early in my Army officer career in Germany. About once a quarter, the U.S. Army Europe commander, then a three-star general, called a maintenance meeting and directed that every single battalion commander and his maintenance support team drive to Stuttgart (for me, it was a three-hour trip from Nurnberg). There were easily 75 or a hundred people sitting in the room with the commanders in front and their staff behind them.

No matter what, the general was *always* late by at least ten or fifteen minutes. I believe it gave him some sense of egotistical power to know so many were waiting for him. Then, for hours on end, he would go over almost every single item of non-operational equipment in the command and ask detailed questions about part numbers and status. He rarely let a commander go without "drawing blood"—finally asking a question the commander and staff could not answer. He would humiliate them and go to the next victim. Not once was my presence really needed, and I thought of the hundreds of thousands of taxpayer dollars wasted in a meeting with a micromanaging but intellectually brilliant commander, who loved the power of being a "snoopervisor." Unfortunately, his poor leadership was not discovered, and he was selected for a fourth star.

2. Democratic Leadership Style

This style is more participative in nature, and the leader involves team members in making critical decisions. It works well for an organization where team members are highly skilled and experienced. This style is also called participative leadership and requires the leader to be intelligent, creative, considerate, and competent. It typically requires a leader with a high EQ (emotional quotient) versus a high IQ (intelligence quotient). It also requires restraint and patience. With this style, results normally take longer to achieve, but as individuals and teams build confidence and competence, effectiveness increases. It takes longer for the results to taper off compared to autocratic styles.

However, keep in mind that there may come a time when the team's performance begins to taper off as people become more complacent and satisfied and settle for things as they are. This is where the leader may need to switch to a little more autocratic or charismatic leadership to inject new energy and direction. In most workplace scenarios, a democratic leadership style is preferred over other leadership styles.

3. Coaching Leadership Style

This style can be one of the most effective leadership styles. Here, the leader doesn't lead directly but indirectly. These leaders are more like coaches or teachers and concentrate on developing others through mentoring and coaching team members. It is a relatively modern leadership style and often comes with a bouquet of additional benefits such as boosting employee motivation, increasing their performance skills, grooming, and motivating team members.

One of the most important jobs of any leader is to replace themselves and develop a future cadre of skilled, competent, emerging leaders for future promotion. In one Fortune 500 company, a leader cannot hope to be promoted until they have developed a competent replacement and coached and developed them to take their place.

I wrote about the autocratic, dictatorial army general in his maintenance meeting. I will offer a comparative example. After I retired from the Army, I was invited to return to Germany to attend a leadership conference led by the four-star Commanding General of Africa Command (AFRICOM), General Kip Ward, headquartered in Germany. I sat next to him for two full days while he received briefings from numerous leaders concerning progress and issues in Africa. For two full days, Ward sat and *listened.* He rarely asked a question or made suggestions or comments. He simply took notes and showed deep respect and interest in each presenter. This created a very safe, open, synergistic culture in the room, and people were free to ask questions and make comments. Finally, near the end, he stood and asked more questions and gave what the Army terms his "commander's intent" and guidance. It was an impressive display of a non-egotistical leader at his best. Ward also demonstrated the next style: strategic leadership.

4. Strategic Leadership Style

According to Wikipedia, *"Strategic leadership is the ability to influence others to voluntarily make decisions that enhance the prospects for the organization's long-term success."* The key word here is long-term. A strategic leader must be able to express a strategic vision for the organization and persuade others to pursue that vision with the help of correct strategies and tools. Strategic leaders create teams of team members who are well-trained and well-equipped to deal with unforeseen risks and threats.

This style is one which can be integrated into other styles of leadership. It is also very important in senior or executive leadership roles. Of all the styles, this is the most learned and developed, typically over much time and experience. It requires a very open mind, curiosity, and a willingness to explore new horizons. It is also rarely the place for autocracy.

5. Transformational Leadership Style

This is a leadership style that focuses on creating a transformation in an organization. It is not a quick-fix style and typically takes time. Transformational leaders create a thriving work culture through effective communication and a certain level of strategic vision and intellectual stimulation to initiate change in oneself and others in an organization.

Transformational leadership focuses on setting high goals with strict deadlines and working in unison to accomplish them on time. Transformational leaders set challenging expectations for themselves and the team to achieve exceptional results. Therefore, it sometimes has elements of both autocratic and democratic leadership.

6. Laissez-faire Leadership Style

The literal meaning of the French word *laissez-faire* is "allow to do" which can be translated as "let it be" in English. Leaders delegate the responsibility to team members and let them work independently with minimum or no interference, giving the maximum scope for innovation and flexibility. It fits best for creative teams with self-motivated and experienced individuals who don't require a high level of supervision.

Mahatma Gandhi was a laissez-faire leader who believed that people work best when they are not told what to do but encouraged to work on their own. One story that illustrates this happened when he was a leader of a community. It was agreed that everyone would share equally in the work of the community, including the odorous job of cleaning the latrines. Gandhi's name came up, and his wife vehemently opposed, pointing out pridefully that they were the leaders and should not bend to such menial tasks. He said nothing, and quietly went out to clean the latrines. She soon joined him. This story also lends itself to the next style: charismatic leadership.

7. Charismatic Leadership Style

Leaders applying a charismatic leadership style are the ones who attract a plethora of people with their personality and charisma. An example might be President John F. Kennedy. Sadly, and oppositely, Adolf Hitler was another. They are self-motivated, passionate, and confident, with an almost magnetic ability to draw others to them or their cause.

This style can build a powerful standing in the marketplace and gain a huge fan following. Many celebrities and movie stars manage to do this and become social and political influencers, even in subjects they know little about. Ghandi, in the latrine story, was totally different from the charismatic Kennedy, but he still drew others to him by the power of his quiet, charismatic example. The Indian Prime Minister Narendra Modi, first elected in May 2014, has recently been considered as one of the more charismatic leaders in the world.

However, on the flip side, success or failure heavily relies on the leader and his or her impact. It is perceived as more of a one-person show than a collective team effort. When the leader is absent, so is his or her influence.

"You can get by on charm for about 15 minutes. After that, you better know something." —H. Jackson Brown, Jr.

Leadership Is Example. Example Is Leadership.

No matter which of the above styles is used, almost all of them depend on the personal example of the leader. People tend to respect and trust leaders who "lead from the front" and are willing to roll up their sleeves and do the mucky, hard work. I refer to this as "muddy-boots leadership."

The president of Amazon, Jeff Bezos, was once seen wearing a T-shirt, working alongside his dock workers, and loading container ships during a walk-out period by dock workers.

"You don't lead people by what you say to them; you lead them by what they see you do. True leaders are self-leaders . . . . Leadership is an art expressed by the demonstration of characters worthy of imitation, emulation, and inspiration. It is neither a title nor a position." —Israelmore Ayivor, Ghanaian author, teacher, and preacher

Great, truly effective leaders set the example in their own morals, values, and lives. They walk the talk and represent and even epitomize the values and expectations they set for others. Here are more stories about the power of example:

General George S. Patton was a flamboyant, charismatic, and normally autocratic leader. He was either loved or despised by his subordinates and by the American people and press. However, he possessed an extraordinary aura of self-confidence and personal courage and was very charismatic. He demonstrated this early in his career in World War I and carried it forward into World War II.

In the early months of the war, American soldiers were facing a strong enemy in North Africa. A story is told of an instance where critical ammunition was waiting in landing craft offshore, requiring foot soldiers to wade into the surf and carry the ammo boxes to waiting trucks inland. However, enemy planes were periodically strafing the beach with machine gun fire. Soldiers reactively hunkered down in hastily dug foxholes, uncertain what to do.

Patton was riding along the beach in a Jeep, saw the situation in a glance and acted. He calmly waded out into the surf, put two boxes of ammunition on his shoulders and marched up the shore to the trucks. He then returned and did it again. Soldiers asked each other, "Who is that guy?" Then they saw the stars on Patton's helmet. "Hey, that's the Old Man . . . That's Patton!"

The soldiers quickly followed Patton's example while also repelling the enemy planes with effective fire. One account says that Patton stayed out in the surf for several hours, working alongside his soldiers.

He knew that no strategic battle plan in his mind or on paper would work if the brave soldiers fighting inland had no ammunition.

Later, Patton was criticized by a war correspondent who wondered why a general would be doing such grunt work. Patton said, "Eighty percent of my personal mission is to inspire morale in my soldiers."

Interestingly, he demonstrated this "muddy boots leadership" early on in his career as a tank company commander in World War I. He could be seen atop his turret, bullets whizzing around him, as he led and inspired his tank crews from the front.

Another amazing example of personal battlefield leadership comes from the history of young Alexander the Great. Alexander was a skilled warrior and an extremely charismatic and visionary leader who expanded his empire across much of the then-known world. In 325 BCE, Alexander and his men lay siege to the walled city of Mallian in pre-modern Pakistan. The Mallian citadel was substantial, with walls a mile in circumference. Alexander's team was able to force open one of the gates and make their way into the outer parts of the citadel. His Macedonians then began to undermine the next layer of walls.

Alexander quickly became impatient at the pace of the siege, so he grabbed a ladder and went up the wall himself. He was followed by only two soldiers. The rest of the soldiers, nervous about the safety of their king, crowded to get up the ladders so that they could protect him. There were too many of them, and the ladders collapsed under the weight. So, there was Alexander, alone, standing on top of the walls. The Mallians soon realized this was Alexander, the Macedonian leader, and focused their energies on him. His soldiers begged him to jump down to safety in their arms, but he refused.

Instead, Alexander leaped into the inner area of the citadel, fighting valiantly alone, surrounded by enemy soldiers. There, he killed the Mallians' leader before an arrow penetrated Alexander's lung, and he was severely wounded. Seeing the courage and example of their general, the soldiers aggressively renewed their attack, mounted new ladders, and leapt down to find him. They found Alexander, surrounded by the dead enemy he had killed, and carried him away for surgery. He nearly died from the surgery but propped himself up in a boat so his soldiers could see him and gain the courage for the rest of the successful campaign.

The tide of history has been turned by leaders showing exemplary courage on the front lines, such as Colonel Joshua Chamberlain's leadership at Little Round Top at Gettysburg in the American Civil War. Chamberlain's men were positioned to guard the extreme left flank of the Union Army. As the battle wore on, his unit ran out of ammunition. Realizing his regiment would likely be overrun by the advancing rebels, Chamberlain gave the command, "Fix Bayonets." He led a bayonet change into the advancing enemy causing them to break and run. For this act of bravery, he received the Congressional Medal of Honor.

Another example was General George Washington's personal example and courage throughout the American War of Independence. One notable experience was when Washington led his struggling army in the winter of 1776 to cross the Delaware River and conduct a surprise attack on the British. His men defeated the British forces of Hessian troops in Trenton, New Jersey. This victory is credited with giving the colonies a much-needed victory and showing they could defeat the British.

Examples of this kind of leader in business and religion abound. In the early days of Microsoft, Bill Gates would go into the company cafeteria, sometimes at two or three in the morning, and sit down with staff members. He would talk with them, ask their opinions and share his vision.

I have been particularly impressed with the leadership style of Torstein Hagen, the president of Viking Cruise lines. He is often found wandering the decks of his ships or standing at the dock on sail-away. He is glad-handing, thanking, and even rolling up his sleeves to help. He attributes this attitude to the hard work ethic he learned from his parents when he was growing up on a farm in Norway. He chooses to be "where the game is played."

It was Jesus Christ who told his followers, "Come, follow me" (Luke 18:22 KJV). Christ repeatedly set the example, such as in healing the sick or showing compassion to the woman taken in adultery.

These stories, and dozens of others of exemplary leaders, illustrate how important it is for leaders to not distance themselves from the front lines and show personal commitment, passion, engagement, and courage in whatever the mission is. Too many leaders hide out in their offices, excusing their absenteeism through constant involvement in the strategic and operational aspects of their roles.

I once saw a funny cartoon of an obese CEO walking through the work area and saying, "Keep up the good work, whoever you are and whatever you are doing." This lack of presence among their workforce will eventually hurt their bottom line. They will pay a price for it.

Finally, leadership can emerge from just about anyone. A favorite example comes from the magnificent movie and book *The Boys in the Boat*. "Rowing as one" was the big lesson that star rower Joe Rants learned. In effect, there are not eight men in the boat—there is only one in the form of eight. The coach made it crystal clear: "If you are not one, you are not mine; at least you do not have a seat in my boat."

I liked this quote from the book: "Rowing is a sport of fundamental paradoxes. For one thing, an eight-oared racing shell—powered by unusually large and physically powerful men or women—is commanded, controlled, and directed by the smallest and least powerful person in the boat. The coxswain must have the force of character to look men or women twice his or her size in the face, bark orders at them, and be confident that the leviathans will respond instantly and unquestioningly to those orders. It is perhaps the most incongruous relationship in sports."

We may never know the full extent of extraordinary leadership moments. One of the observers of the 1936 Olympic race said, quoting from the book, "Standing there, watching them, it occurred to me that when Hitler watched Joe and the boys fight their way back from the rear of the field to sweep ahead of Italy and Germany seventy-five years ago, he saw, but did not recognize, heralds of his doom. He could not have known that one day hundreds of thousands of boys just like them, boys who shared their essential natures—decent and unassuming, not privileged or favored by anything in particular, just loyal, committed, and perseverant—would return to Germany dressed in olive drab, hunting him."

Beware of Your Ego!

The biggest danger of all in any of these leadership styles may be personal egos. *Never let egos get in the way of doing what is right for your team.* When leaders allow their egos or self-serving agendas to override what needs to be done for the health and future of the organization, the ship can easily crash into the rocks or become dead in the water. In my experience, it is most often found in autocratic leaders who draw personal worth from the ability to control others. However, it can manifest itself in any of the styles. *Egos and self-interest erode trust.*

The Stool Analogy

Daniel Gannon said, "Leadership is action, not position." Ultimately, whatever style suits you, getting important things done (action) is the measure of great leadership. However, I have an important caveat.

Whenever you contemplate taking action, stop and consider how to balance the four legs of a symbolic stool: right thing, right time, right way, and right motive. The action will work as hoped only when all four are grounded and balanced. Sometimes, we as leaders are so focused on doing the right thing that we don't stop and ask if it is the right time to do it or if it is the right way to do it. We also need to carefully examine our motives.

I will give you a personal example. As a young captain in the U.S. Army, I often worked long hours, leaving my wife and four children at home. I felt guilty for being absent in their lives so often. So, one day, I rushed in just as dinner was on the table and said, "Hey, let's all go to see the new Disney movie tonight." Of course, this put all the children in an excited hover, unable to finish eating. My wife gave me "The Look" that told me I had made a mistake. I did not know that we had teacher and classroom visits that night for two of the children. So, imagine the letdown that followed. Using the stool analogy, it was possible that going as a family to the movie was the right *thing*, but it was certainly not the right *time*. Because I did not confer with my wife ahead of time, it was the wrong *way*.

But beneath it was perhaps my guilty "stinky cheese" reason or *motive* of wanting to make up for my absenteeism.

So, remember **STOP**: **S**top, **T**ake a breath, **O**bserve the situation and emotions, and **P**roceed with respect and caution.

Make sure you are doing the right thing at the right time, in the right way, *and* with the right motive. (The movie date was very fun two evenings later!)

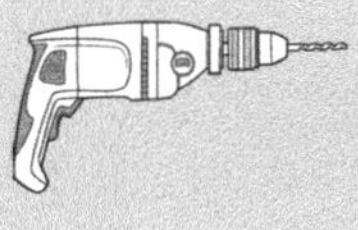

Tool Time!

Do more LBWA—Leadership by Wandering Around: This is one of the most powerful tools to become a more influential, engaged leader. It's so easy to get so caught up in the whirlwind of the job that leaders get stuck behind their desks or off and running to meetings.

Try other styles or be increasingly flexible in how you lead, depending on the situation and the maturity and skill of the team. You may adjust your style over time. Perhaps you will start with autocratic to get a fast start, and then evolve into more democratic or even laissez-faire style.

Set aside a good block of time each day to LBWA. Simply walk around visiting people and engaging with them on a personal basis. *Never use this time to correct or find fault.* Praise them for the work they are doing or their past performance. Learn about their families, hobbies, and interests and share yours with them. At times, you can ask some questions more related to work.

A few good LBWA questions are:

1. How are you doing?
2. What are you learning?
3. What does the team need to learn?
4. What can I do differently to help you do your job better?
5. Is there something frustrating to you about your job that I could be aware of?
6. What is something we can do differently as a team to better serve our customers? (Note the importance of using the word "differently," rather than "better." It is emotionally safer, and you will get much better feedback.)

I'll conclude this chapter with a thought by Warren Bennis: "One of the greatest myths is that somehow leadership is innate or born in: that you either have certain leadership traits or you do not. In fact, the opposite is true: leaders are made not born."

Let us proceed to learn more about how we all can become greater, more influential leaders with the new skills introduced in the Helm Model. Let's start with the first handle **Envision**.

CHAPTER FIVE

Envisioning

The Power of the North Star

One of the most shocking moments in U.S. Olympic history occurred on the rifle range in the 2004 Athens Summer Olympics. Twenty-three-year-old Matthew Emmons had already captured the 50m rifle prone gold medal (even when he had to borrow a teammate's rifle when his had been deliberately sabotaged). He was heavily favored to win the gold in the 50m three position rifle final, and his first two shots were almost perfect. He was so far ahead of the other competitors that all he had to do was place his bullet anywhere in the inner ring of the target to seal his gold medal. He prepared himself, paused his breathing, and took aim. He pulled the trigger. The bullet passed right through the bull's-eye. However, he was puzzled when the tone indicating a hit didn't sound. Matthew then realized that the bull's-eye he had hit was on the wrong target. He dropped from first place to eighth.

This clearly illustrates how critical it is for us to put our sights on the right target, be it in business or our personal lives. *No matter how technically elegant we are, it means nothing if we are not envisioning and focusing on the right vision or goal.*

Where there is no vision, the people perish. —Proverbs 29:18

I have often thought about Proverbs 29:18, particularly as it applies to our lives, our families, and organizations. There are many ways people can "die." We might think mainly of physical death, and this is certainly true. You've probably heard the statement that one of the peak times for people to die physically is within the first six months after retirement. The retirement party is over, and they go home. Suddenly they are left without the fulfillment and purpose they once felt at work. Rather than changing their vision, they simply begin to shut down. That is why Dr. Stephen R. Covey advised never to retire to *leisure* but to retire to *projects.*

I wrote previously that Covey taught that human beings have four critically important dimensions. We are physical, mental, emotional, and spiritual beings and each part of our nature has specific needs. He lined those up with the four needs of human beings: to live (physical), to learn (mental), to love (emotional), and to live for a purpose (spiritual). But perhaps the strongest of these four drivers can be our spirits that need to focus on a purpose or the vision for which we were born to achieve. Finding this purpose invigorates our spirits, igniting power in our minds, hearts, and bodies.

This concept of the spirit within us is found in every major religion I have encountered. It is even among people who do not have a religion. Most people sense something deeper within themselves without necessarily having a religious grounding.

Continuing with this thought, organizations also have a physical, mental, emotional, and spiritual component. Traditional HR and management systems and their ideas tend to concentrate on the physical by providing people with adequate pay and other external monetary bonuses and compensation. They neglect to pay equal attention to the emotional, mental, and spiritual complements of the human beings working for them. Great organizations make sure that their vision ignites and empowers every dimension of their employees.

Thus, it is very possible that people can retire in pieces. Perhaps you have met people who retired their minds, their spirits, and their emotions years ago. The body stayed at work because of the Social Security number and a paycheck. As I wrote earlier, work becomes, in essence, a sort of day prison where the body is admitted at eight and freed from this prison at five o'clock!

I heard a funny ditty playing on the radio station this week. They played a slow-moving funeral march and said eight o'clock and then a fast-moving exciting, invigorating tune and said five o'clock. You can see this in humans as they drag their feet coming into work in the morning. Then, when the bell rings at five, they come alive and rush out to go or do whatever has greater meaning to them, whether it is the pickleball court, their home, or, even more telling, perhaps a bar where they swap horror stories about their boss or job.

As we approach this concept of envisioning, we must ask ourselves: does this vision and mission invigorate not just the body but also the mind, heart, and spirit? There was an article in a major business magazine many years ago inviting people to create a great mission, and the article's title was "You Will Know It When You Tremble."

This happened to me as a young man when I was considering becoming an army officer. I was told that the mission of the army was "to fight and win our nation's wars." When I read this, I thought of my father leaving his home in 1944 to fight in the Pacific and coming home many months later. I felt my heart, mind, and spirit resonate with the Army's mission and to those who gave the ultimate sacrifice to bring our country to peace and freedom. And I thought, "I can do that. I can help fight and win our nation's wars." It was something that resonated with my mind, my body, my heart, and my spirit, and it kept me going. The full Army mission statement today is *"To fight and win our Nation's wars, by providing prompt, sustained land dominance, across the full range of military operations and the spectrum of conflict, in support of combatant commanders."*

If I were to rewrite it, I would shorten it to the following: *To fight and win our Nation's wars by providing prompt sustained land warfare dominance.*

Creating a truly invigorating mission and vision is not merely an intellectual exercise. Nor can it be done in a vacuum by senior leaders in an offsite and then handed out at an enthusiastic meeting at the beginning of the year. Too often those kinds of statements end up as what Covey calls "framed whatever" hanging on the walls, never referred to again or even known by the people in the organization.

I sometimes prove this point when I work with senior leadership teams while secretly holding a squirt gun behind my back. I was working with a company in Park City, Utah, and I asked the organizational leaders, "Do you have a mission statement?"

They all proudly nodded. I then pointed the squirt gun at the president and asked, "What is it?"

He looked a little sheepish and mumbled a couple of words and I squirted him (lightly, of course!). Everyone else laughed until I squirted the rest to make my point. The funny thing is the secretary was the only person who could remember the mission statement. She was sitting in the back taking notes when she raised her hand and said, "I know what it is!"

She had typed it enough and made enough viewgraphs and PowerPoint slides in her career to remember it. Point made!

This example is by no means an aberration. One study by the Harris Group has shown that only about 15% of people in any organization can accurately identify the vision or mission or even the current goals of the organization they work for! I find that figure holds true in the culture surveys I use with my clients and may even be too high in many cases. (If you want to prove this for yourself, see if you can accurately write your organization's mission statement in the margin of this page!)

An inspiring mission or vision can be extremely powerful when an organization develops one with input from many people and then widely publishes and uses it. It becomes the basis for all decision-making, organization belonging, and even advancement and recognition. We will explore this process further in the next chapter on enrolling.

In 2009, Daniel Pink wrote an extraordinarily fascinating book about human motivation. It is called *Drive: The Surprising Truth of What Motivates Us*. What I enjoy the most about his book is how well he has documented his findings with on-the-ground research worldwide. I highly recommend you watch an extremely entertaining video on YouTube from Daniel Pink called "RSA Animate: Drive." Pink debunks and disproves the concept that money is the primary motivator for people—that the more you pay people, the harder they will work. He found that, in most cases, the opposite is true. Instead, he found three things that are the strongest motivators in releasing human potential at work and in life. The first of these was giving them a **compelling purpose**. The other two were **self-actualization**—the opportunity to give and bring the best of themselves to their purpose—and **self-mastery**—the opportunity to learn, grow, develop, and improve without the shackles of micromanagement.

So, how do we create this vision, mission, and purpose for our organizations?

I'm going to refer to this as the North Star. In the Northern Hemisphere, the North Star is the one star that does not move. It stays stable while the other constellations slowly revolve around it. Mariners have used the North Star to position themselves at sea and guide them in their journey from the beginning of time. People have used the North Star as a guide on land as well. Navigators in the Southern Hemisphere use the constellation called the Southern Cross to stay oriented. Just like these navigators, every organization needs a symbolic North Star to guide them. We need one as individuals and in marriages, families, and personal relationships.

But it serves no purpose if it is vague, wordy, cumbersome, and filled with jargon. Nor is it of any value if it hangs on the wall and is not used to make any significant decisions ("framed whatever").

This is the most important starting point in the leadership journey of this book. This compelling purpose drives the other elements of the Helm Model: enroll, enable, engage, and explore. And an inspiring purpose also builds trust. The North Star includes more than the vision, mission, values, and measures of success. It also drives the *strategy*.

The bottom line is that the *why* drives the *what*. This is solidly proven in Simon Sinek's great book *Start with Why*. This North Star should be referred to whenever a decision is made or a tempting offer arrives on the table.

An old Arab Proverb says, "The eagle that chases two rabbits catches neither." Shakespeare noted in *The Merchant of Venice*, "All that glitters is not gold." I often turn this around when consulting organizations and remind them that all that glitters is not goal! It is painfully obvious that the more goals we chase, the fewer we can accomplish with excellence and accuracy. Returning to our North Star helps us decide what we should and should not do.

Tim Cook, the CEO of Apple, once said, "Every day Apple says no to good ideas, and every week, we say no to great ideas so we can stay focused on what we do best. Every product Apple makes will fit on the desk in front of you, and last year, we made billions of dollars." He took this cue from Steve Jobs himself, who said, "People think focus means saying yes to the thing you've got to focus on. But that's not what it means at all. It means saying no to the hundred other good ideas that there are. You have to pick carefully. I'm actually as proud of the things we haven't done as the things I have done. Innovation is saying 'no' to 1,000 things."

Having a compelling North Star also helps make tough decisions in other ways. I heard an anecdote once about a decision that Disneyland had to make. For several years, Disneyland would close the park to the public at 8 o'clock and then re-open it for special groups from organizations and companies. When I grew up, I always looked forward to when our church sold tickets for a special night at Disneyland.

One day, Disney received a request from a group to have an LGBTQ+ night at Disneyland. Disney leaders knew that approving this would result in opposition from some people and organizations. As they figured out what to do, they returned to their North Star. At that time, their mission statement was to the effect of *"We create happiness by providing the finest in entertainment for people of all ages everywhere."*

They realized that the answer lay in their purpose statement. Denying this legally recognized organization the opportunity to be happy at Disneyland would mean they would have to begin adding asterisks and listing various organizations that could *not* be happy at

Disneyland. They decided to allow the organization to have a night at Disneyland. Sure enough, they got push-back from some organizations who urged their people to boycott Disneyland for appearing to support the LGBTQA lifestyle. All that aside, I give them high marks for using their North Star for its very purpose: to drive strategy and decisions, not just the monetary bottom line.

The following illustration provides a map for this process from macro to micro.

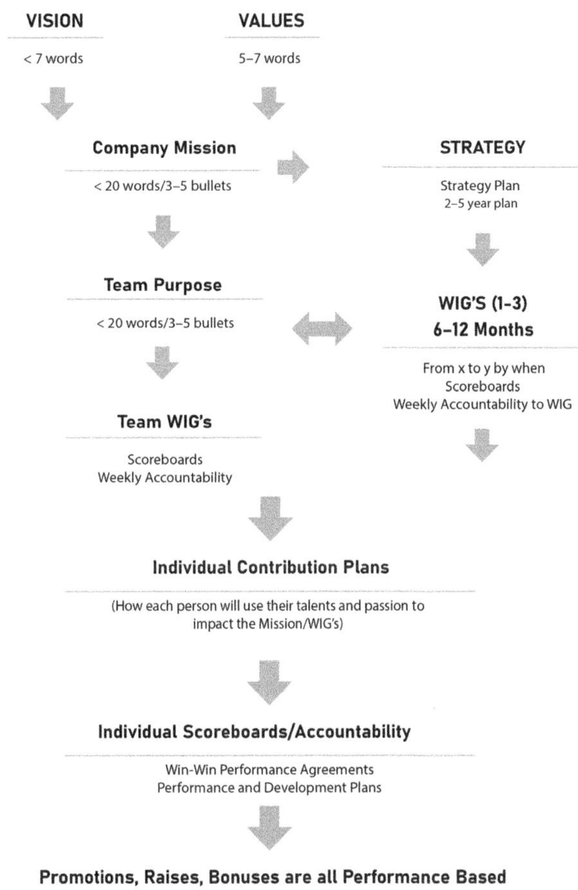

We start at the top with vision, values, company mission, and team purpose statements. These together constitute the "why." The arrows down and to the right drive the "how" of strategy. The strategic plan is a two- to five-year plan. It then drives down into WIG's (Wildly Important Goals), bite-sized chunks of the strategic plan that can be completed in less than a year. Ideally, they all drive down to everyone, from the CEO to the front line, creating their supporting individual contribution plans for the year. These become the basis for accountability, promotions, raises, and bonuses.

I have spent years as a consultant helping organizations achieve what is in this illustration. It is astounding how few really understand and apply this powerful process of aligning individual and personal contributions with the goals, strategy, and an overarching purpose of the organization.

The result of the envisioning or missioning process should be to create four main statements:

- **A Vision Statement:** A vision statement is very short and defines what the result will be if you consistently live out and execute your mission. The U.S. Airforce once had a vision statement, *"Global Power, Global Reach."* A company I work with produces buckets of sweet, nutrient licks for livestock. Their vision is *"A Healthier World through Healthier Animals."* Note that a vision statement does not dive into what you do or produce, just the high-level outcome.
- **A Mission Statement:** This statement should be no more than fifteen words in length (plus additional supporting bullets) and should be inspiring. It briefly includes enough for people to know what it is you provide. It can even include elements from the vision statement. For example, *"We create a healthier world by providing quality, innovative delivery of vitamins and nutrients to livestock."*

Our mission statement at VisionBound is *"We accelerate greatness by releasing human potential."*

- **A Team Purpose Statement:** Keep in mind that you want only one main mission statement for your company or organization. It becomes confusing when there are a plethora of mission statements floating around. Solve this by having individual teams, divisions, departments, or directorates create supporting team purpose statements, following the fifteen-word maximum rule. The key is to tie your teams together with some unifying wording. An example of a team purpose statement for the marketing team in VisionBound might be, *"We accelerate greatness and release potential through marketing to a growing number of teams and individuals world-wide."*

- **A Values Statement or List:** This statement or list outlines the core values of your company. These values can be means values (honesty, integrity) or ends values (reputation, quality). There should be no more than seven. If you can make them spell an acronym, all the better.
- **Measures of Success:** This important piece defines how you can tell if you are successful or not. These measures must be number-based and measurable. They should be constantly monitored, score-boarded, and instantly available. Examples could be:
    - net profit
    - gross sales
    - new customers gained
    - cost of goods sold
    - average sales per customer
    - post-operative disease reduction

Here are some rules for envisioning the vision and mission:

- Keep it short.
- Keep it inspiring and compelling.
- Involve many in its creation.
- Publish it widely and refer to it often.

Keep it Short: Keep a mission statement well under 15 words. The wording on Disneyland's former mission statement illustrates this: *"We create happiness by providing the finest in entertainment to people of all ages everywhere."* (fifteen words)

The best way to start is to look deeply at the why behind the what of your products or services. Harvard professor Theodore Levitt once made a remarkable statement: "People don't want a quarter-inch *drill.* They want a quarter-inch *hole.*" What is the real hole that your company's products or services fill? Great salespeople sell *solutions*, not *products*. They listen carefully to what the customer really wants before offering solutions. For example, when I worked with a sales team in an automotive dealership, I advised them to delve deeply into the exact needs they want their car to fill. If it is a car for a new teenage driver, the needs will be different than a car for a large family.

The reason mission statements become wordy, cumbersome, and unmemorable is because they are often designed by a committee where everyone wants to get their words and ideas in the statement. It's easy to write something longer; writing it shorter takes much more thought and effort. Every word needs to be powerful, and the result needs to be extremely short.

Keep it Inspiring and Compelling: As mentioned previously, an excellent article that discusses creating powerful mission statements is called "You Will Know It When You Tremble." If you read the mission statement and it does not make you inwardly tremble, you might not yet be where you need to be.

Let me illustrate this with a project I did for a major insurance company in Australia. Their mission statement was long and wordy and completely missed the point of why people buy insurance. When we dug deeper into it, we realized that the ultimate purpose of insurance is to provide peace of mind in the event of a car accident, home or natural disaster, or death itself.

We brainstormed it for several hours, and the result really did make us tremble: *We provide peace of mind by protecting the things you love.*

When we introduced it to the rest of the company, their excitement and passion awoke. They used this mission statement as they should. It became a basis for everything, even for customer sales and service. They displayed it on the walls of their offices. Now, when customers come in the door, instead of hard-selling insurance, they start by referring to their mission statement and asking, *"What do you love that needs protecting?"* The results have been immediate and measurable. Their top agent told me they increased their sales significantly. This story illustrates how a compelling purpose awakens the passion of even the sales staff because they know what they are really providing.

Sometimes, mission statements also lead to creating a memorable, short slogan. One I admire can be found on the side of large Old Dominion freight trucks: *Helping the World Keep Promises.* Imagine how that might motivate a driver on his long-haul journeys, knowing that promises are being kept in the back of his truck.

The key is to keep the main part of the mission statement very short and compelling. Start with the *why* that lies beneath what your company offers and does: create happiness, provide peace of mind, keep promises, heal the mind and body, etc. Follow with a few words describing the *how:* "by protecting the things you love."

Now, you can further define the mission with a short list of three to five bullets underneath the main mission statement. For example, the insurance company could include such things as:

- cellar to roof home protection
- new and used automobiles
- intellectual property

Make sure that each bullet is no more than a few words in length. If possible, make these more memorable with an acronym. One hospital team I worked with used CARE as their values: **C**aring, **A**ccessible, **R**esponsive, and **E**mpathetic.

Involve many in its creation: People tend to own that to which they contribute. The process of this is outlined in the following pages.

Publish it widely and refer to it often: The mission statement serves no purpose if it ends up as the "framed whatever" on the wall, unknown or ignored by most. One good idea is to print it on the back of every business card and ensure that every employee has business cards. These business cards then proclaim, "here is who I am, and here is what we do."

Once, I trained an elementary school's staff in Ohio. Each classroom created a class mission statement to hang outside their door. My absolute favorite was from third-grade class: "We come to school to know what everything means. We learn to read so we can read to our children when we grow up. We learn math so we become smart at work and don't get fired." It was handwritten by a student and framed with each student's hand print next to their name. When their smiling teacher greeted the children at the door, each student reached over and slapped their painted hand and name on the poster. A superb example of being envisioned, enrolled, and engaged!

The Process

I suggest a four-step process for creating an inspiring purpose:

- Brainstorm
- Incubate
- Finalize
- Publish

Brainstorm: In this step, involve as many people as possible, including customers. It has been said, "no involvement, no ownership." One of the worst things you can do is take senior leaders off to some offsite retreat and come back with the vision and mission.

Here are some ideas:

1. Send out some questions in a survey to all staff and selected stakeholders. (Contact us at VisionBound for a list of these questions.)
2. Bring together focus groups to discuss their ideas of the purpose, vision, and mission.
3. Bring together a small group of key individuals, with the data above, to brainstorm and create about three sample mission statements, several vision statements, a list of values and measures of success. Write these out on posters or flip charts to use in the voting or incubation step.

Incubate: Post the flip charts and results of the brainstorming group on a wall. Invite everyone in the company to vote on the ones they like the most, and even use Post-it notes to add their suggestions or word changes. For instance, place a "one" on their first choice, followed by "two," etc. They can also place votes on the list of values, placing hash marks or check marks next to the seven or so they like most. Let people add to or vote on the measures of success and the vision statements.

Note that everyone should now feel they were listened to and had input to the survey questions and now the opportunity to vote and buy into the four elements of purpose.

Finalize: The original brainstorming team may now reconvene to score and study the incubation results and assign someone to clean up and process the results by a specified date.

Publish: Publish and disseminate the results widely. The main mission and vision belong on posters, websites, headers, or footers on agendas and documents and, as I mentioned, on the back of business cards. Introduce the vision, mission, values, and measures of success in an important meeting and refer back to them often, even going so far as to periodically recite the mission. Use it in job interviews and performance reviews.

Refer to this mission statement and values often to make important decisions.

In conclusion, envisioning is a powerful and all-essential spoke in the Helm Model. It drives most everything that follows, as we will explore in the next chapter on **Enrolling**.

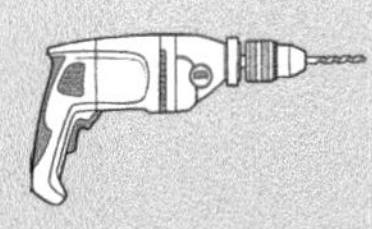

Final Challenge

1. Go forth and work as a team to create a mission statement or team purpose statement.

2. If you have a family, consider writing a family mission statement by involving everyone, especially your children.

3. If you want a guide for writing your personal mission statement, refer to the tools section of www.VisionBound.com.

4. Once finalized, refer to your mission statement often to make decisions.

5. To see more examples of good mission statements tied to customer service, see Tool Number Eight.

CHAPTER SIX

Enrolling

Creating Ownership

In the last chapter, we addressed how important it is to create a compelling vision that ignites the passion and contribution of everyone. Unfortunately, many organizations seem to stop here. Leaders sometimes go off on an offsite and return with a mission statement and strategy. But they rarely do what it takes to truly enroll people in that vision. Soon, it becomes "framed whatever" hanging on the walls.

I mentioned previously that one study found that only 15% of people in the United States can accurately identify the vision, mission, or goals of the organization they are working for. This is because they were never *enrolled.*

Enrolling is a term for getting people physically, mentally, emotionally, and spiritually excited and feeling ownership in the all-important purpose. We want everyone on the ship to know exactly what the North Star is, where to find it, and how to use it in making decisions and creating new ideas for improving the organization.

Enrolling is an ongoing and never-ending process. Sometimes, company leaders think they have enrolled people simply by having a yearly enthusiastic meeting introducing the vision, mission, and strategic plan with fancy PowerPoints and inspiring rhetoric. They walk off the stage, mentally patting themselves on the back, and assume that the people will leave inspired and ready to execute the new plan with vigor and inspiration.

Many people have a rather jaded view of this process because they have seen it come and go year after year. It is important to remember that *people are not enrolled simply because they are told.* Everyone should periodically be brought back, re-engaged, and reminded about the purpose of the organization. This can be done through a process of reminders, story-telling, and constant reinforcement.

I mentioned previously the four dimensions of the whole person's nature: physical, mental, emotional, and spiritual. Each of these dimensions is a powerful component, and each has great potential when they are inspired, energized, and work in concert to create great synergy. When you think about it, every organization also has the same four components. And each has an impact on the all-important culture we addressed earlier.

Let's now address enrolling in a several-step process.

Step One: Hire for Success

Before we can begin enrolling people, getting the right people on board is essential. In his book *Good to Great*, Jim Collins stresses the importance of "getting the right people on the bus," and then getting them on the right *seats* on the bus. By this, he means matching people into positions where they can work best with their talents, passions, and skills. With the right people on board, you can take your ship almost anywhere it needs to go.

There is more information on how to conduct effective interviews in Tool Two in the toolbox section of the book. There, you will see examples of great behavior-based interview questions and learn some ideas on preparing for and conducting effective interviews. These questions will help distinguish the right people for your team and where they might fit best.

Step Two: Onboard Effectively and Immediately

Many years ago, I saw a darling poster of a little kitten, and underneath it were the words, "Things are at their best at their beginning." Anyone who has ever held a newborn baby would probably agree, at least in part, with that statement!

Of course, we know that people can grow, improve, and become better throughout their lives, but there is something magical with the freshness that arrives at any beginning. That is why the process of onboarding is so critical as we enroll people physically, mentally, emotionally, and spiritually in their new jobs.

People tend to arrive on the first day excited to begin their new careers or even their first entry-level job as a teenager. I remember my daughter Rachelle heading off to her first day working at a fast-food restaurant. I remember seeing her bounce out the door wearing her new T-shirt and hat. Unfortunately, because of poor leadership by the store manager, I gradually saw Rachelle's passion and energy sucked out of her. By the end of the summer, she could hardly wait for school to begin so she could quit her job.

Therefore, we want to capture, focus, and maintain that initial energy that people arrive with. The very first hours are crucial, and many things need to be done during that very first day and week.

When I started my army career as a platoon leader in Germany, I remember my First Sergeant saying that when a new soldier arrives in the unit, leadership has three precious days to get him or her fully engaged and feeling important and needed to the Army and the unit. Suppose these inspiring and important things do not happen initially. In that case, the soldier may instead be gladly and dangerously "recruited and onboarded" by the "barracks rats"—troublemaking, negative soldiers with a bad attitude who are always looking to drag a new victim down with them and perhaps even get them involved in drugs or drinking. Nearly every organization has these kinds of people.

Every human being has a deep inner need to belong. We seek and need to fill that longing somewhere or somehow. It is one reason teenagers join gangs. I once heard that "some people would rather be wanted for murder than not wanted at all." As leaders, it is our responsibility and our job to make sure every new employee feels valued and important and welcomed the moment they arrive under our care.

For detailed information on how to onboard effectively, please read Tool Three on onboarding and engaging folks from the start toward the back of the book.

Step Three: Instill an Excitement for the Vision

The previous chapter addressed the importance of vision, mission, values, and strategy. Now, we need to embed it in the hearts, minds, bodies, and spirits of ourselves and our staff. Remember the figure I mentioned previously: studies show that less than 15% of people even know what the mission, vision, strategy, and current goals are or feel that their work is aligned with those goals.

We mentioned in the onboarding process how important it is to enthusiastically and passionately enroll people on day one with the team or company's vision, mission and defining purpose. But when the onboarding is over, reinvigorating people with the purpose is crucial. Jack Welch once said that people should know the purposes and goals of the organization so clearly that you could shake them awake at four in the morning, and they could mumble it correctly in a half-asleep stupor.

There are simple ways to do this.

First, publish it everywhere! Make sure the short and compelling mission statement is posted where it is hard to ignore. A great mission or purpose can ignite ownership in customers, vendors, visitors, and family members.

If you visit the website of Merck, you will see their current mission statement: "To discover, develop and provide innovative products and services that save and improve lives around the world." Not a bad mission statement, even if is seventeen words long. If Merck followed my model, they would turn it around to say, "We save and improve lives around the world by discovering and providing innovative products and services." I would add the word "we" instead of "to" and start with the deeper purpose.

But I read that several years ago, Merck had another short vision statement: *To Alleviate Human Suffering*. It was posted where everyone entering their main building could see it. They were constantly reminded and reinspired about why they were coming to work. I heard from one of their leaders that Merck invented an eyedrop that could cure river blindness in children in Africa, caused by dirty water. The company returned to its purpose, to alleviate human suffering, and distributed at no cost millions of vials of the medicine to families unable to afford it. That is an example of staying enrolled in the company's purpose. It would also serve as an inspiring story to everyone working there.

Second, create symbols. A picture can be worth a thousand words, and most people are very visual in how they process and remember information. Symbolizing your company in its logo or other images can be very helpful in keeping people reminded and enrolled.

There is a well-known story about a janitor at NASA who, when asked by President John F. Kennedy what his job was, responded, "I'm helping put a man on the moon." Of course, this says something about the individual himself, but it also says a great deal about the leadership and the purpose-driven culture around him. President Kennedy clearly stated this purpose in 1961 when he said:

> I believe that this nation should commit itself to achieving the goal, before this decade is out, of landing a man on the moon and returning him safely to the earth. No single space project in this period will be more impressive to mankind, or more important for the long-range exploration of space; and none will be so difficult or expensive to accomplish . . . . But in a very real sense, it will not be one man going to the moon—if we make this judgment affirmatively, it will be an entire nation. For all of us must work to put him there.

Step Four: Help Them Create a Personal Vision and Action Plan

Clear job descriptions can help people understand where they fit into the overall organization, particularly if the job description ties in closely to the vision and mission. Once people know and feel mentally, physically, and emotionally aligned to the mission and vision, take the next step by helping each person create their own Individual Contribution Plan or ICP. Ideally, this can happen in the first weeks of being hired.

Begin the ICP with the summary of the vision, mission, and strategy I outlined at the end of the previous chapter. This ICP process can start with the new hires writing how they see their role contributing to the vision and mission and why they strongly believe in it. Then, help them identify their unique talents and gifts that can contribute significantly to achieving the vision. Imagine that you are holding a glass of water, and when you release it, you leave your fingerprints on that glass. No one else in the world has that same set of prints. This can also be true of each person working on a team: each can, and likely wants to, leave their unique fingerprints on the team.

One way you can help them is to interview each person, using the leadership interview questions found in the Toolbox. It is likely that those you interview may never have thought deeply about some of the questions, and as you gently inquire, you can help them uncover ways they can best contribute.

Step Five: Recognize, Encourage, and Reward the Right Behaviors

I will address this in more detail in the chapter on Engaging. Remember the axiom: "you get what you allow, and you get what you recognize and reward." If you allow people to come to work late and gossipy, you will get gossipy, late people. Be engaged with your constituents to know what they are doing and how it is aligning with the vision and mission. Recognize, appreciate, and even reward people for these positive, aligned behaviors, and you will get more of these behaviors until they become a part of the culture.

Often in my consulting, I hear people say something to the effect of, "I do 99 things right and hear nothing positive about any of it, but, boy, if I do one thing wrong, they are all over my back." This is a formula to cause deep disengagement and disenrollment.

In conclusion, by enrolling people, you guide them in becoming physically, mentally, emotionally, and even spiritually aligned to the vision, mission, values, and goals of the organization or their team. It creates an inner excitement and growing passion and aligns their efforts with a higher purpose.

But from here, they need the next spoke in our helm: **Enabling**.

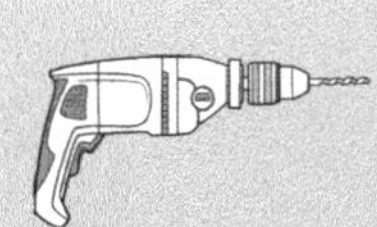

Now it's time to go to work.

Contact us to launch a free Vital Signs Survey throughout your organization. This survey will assess how deeply people are enrolled in your mission, vision, and values. It also delves into motivation and other important factors.

Create focus groups to brainstorm ideas on how to create more enrollment and engagement. Empower those groups to carry out some of their initiatives.

CHAPTER SEVEN

Enabling

Providing the Wind

"When we try to motivate someone without training them, we only frustrate them." —Jack Welch

The full complement of our crew members, each doing their own role, keeps our ship on target. No amount of leadership, vision, or strategy matters if the mechanics can't keep the engines running smoothly.

I have sailed over 100 times on cruise ships. Most of those times, I was on board as a guest lecturer. This put me in contact with senior staff and the ship's captain. Generally, I was hardly aware of the captain's leadership on the bridge, but I was heavily influenced by my room stewards and the quality of the meals produced by the cooks. This goes to show that some of the most influential people in an organization are those who are paid the least and are barely recognized for their contributions. In some places, if the mayor of a town didn't show up for a week, few would notice. But try that with the sanitation team!

In some ways, I would rather be ignorant of and disenrolled to my company's vision, mission, and strategy than excited about it and then be disabled by micromanagement, cumbersome and bureaucratic processes, and a lack of critical resources.

This happened to me a couple of decades ago when, after retiring from the Army, I took a position as the professional development manager at a major university. I arrived excited and hopeful, strongly believing in the inspiring mission of the school and the slogan "Enter to Learn. Go forth to Serve." I felt that the school had done that for me. It was where I met my future wife, gained a passion for business and learning, earned my commission through a great ROTC program, and was launched into a career. I was eager to return and add my talents and energy to this mission.

Things went well for the first couple of years because my manager, friend, and mentor supported me and gave me much latitude to be creative with little or no micromanagement. He trusted and empowered me. All that quickly changed when he left and was replaced by a woman who I consider the "Queen of Micromanagement." I had to pass every little idea and marketing idea past her. This sucked the energy and enthusiasm out of me. I was disempowered, leading to some resentful behavior. This micromanagement and disempowering eventually led to me leaving and ramping up my own consulting company. (Maybe I should send her a thank-you card!)

When people face this kind of dilemma, they feel trapped, perhaps by the "golden handcuffs" of a regular salary and benefits, or too hesitant to make the break. So, many people either quit and leave, or far worse, they quit and *stay.*

There are many ways someone can quit. People can easily RIP: Retire in Pieces. First, their emotions retire, and they "no longer care." At the same time, they can begin to retire mentally: no new ideas, no creativity. They just plod along doing things the same old way, no longer motivated or caring to challenge the processes or come up with new ideas. The spirit, that inner fire, probably left long ago. The body remains at work because it is attached to the paycheck. If they are breathing and doing the minimum expected of them, they can stay off the radar long enough to retire. (We will cover this in more detail in the chapter on engaging.)

There are a few basic things people need to be enabled at work. This is a partial list of the things we can think of as wind in the sails of our ship:

- effective training
- sufficient funding and financial resources
- efficient and effective systems and processes
- adequate time to do quality, satisfying work
- sufficient challenging goals but not so many to overwhelm
- opportunities to grow, progress, and be promoted if desired
- functional equipment, including IT, communications, and whatever material and equipment is critical for their success
- other materials: raw materials and logistical support
- adequate, timely, and accurate communication
- a reward and recognition system that goes beyond the "institutional atta-boys" tailored to their uniqueness
- superb, inspiring leadership, which is the basis of this book

"Feed down rather than kiss up" is an adage I once heard. Too many leaders and even staff members are focused on kissing up to please or look good to the boss or the system. Instead, spend your time and effort feeding down: give your people the resources they need to succeed. In turn, they will likely perform higher and higher, which may eventually help you succeed. You don't need to wave your flag, kiss up, or patronize anyone. The record of your team will stand on its own merits and so will you.

At home, look for as many ways as you can to enable your children and family members to be productive. Many years ago, my wife created a cleaning caddy with all the tools each child would need to dust and clean their room. This helped them feel ownership and equipped to organize and take care of their personal stewardship of their room. It did not work like magic, but it did help!

In conclusion, we have covered envisioning, enrolling, and enabling. With these spokes behind us, we now turn to the third spoke: *engaging.* **Spoiler alert! It is very hard to engage people who are not envisioned, enrolled, and enabled!**

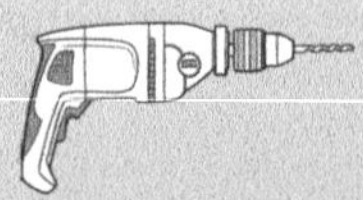

Application Ideas

1. If you would like us to set up a culture survey at no cost for your organization, please contact me at kevin@visionbound.com. The survey questions confidentially drill into all these factors. You might be surprised at what your staff really thinks about what is enabling or disabling them at work.
2. Create action teams to brainstorm ideas on how to better enable people at work.

3. In your family, look for new ways to enable everyone to engage in the work of the home. Have a family brainstorming session to work out ideas.

CHAPTER EIGHT

Engaging

Releasing Potential

This element of the Helm Model best follows the previous three. It is hard to engage people when they have never been enrolled in the vision. **And few things frustrate someone more than to be excited and enrolled only to be disabled.**

What we are doing in this Helm Model is releasing human potential. The world's greatest untapped natural resource is not oil, natural gas, or solar power. *It is human potential.* If we could harness, focus, and release our full human potential, we could solve any problem in any organization, nation, or the world. That's what the Helm Model is all about.

Sadly, people only use a tiny percentage of their full potential at work and even in life. If asked, most people may agree that the average person has more talent, energy, and creativity than their current job enables or even allows them to do. There is a wealth of untapped potential.

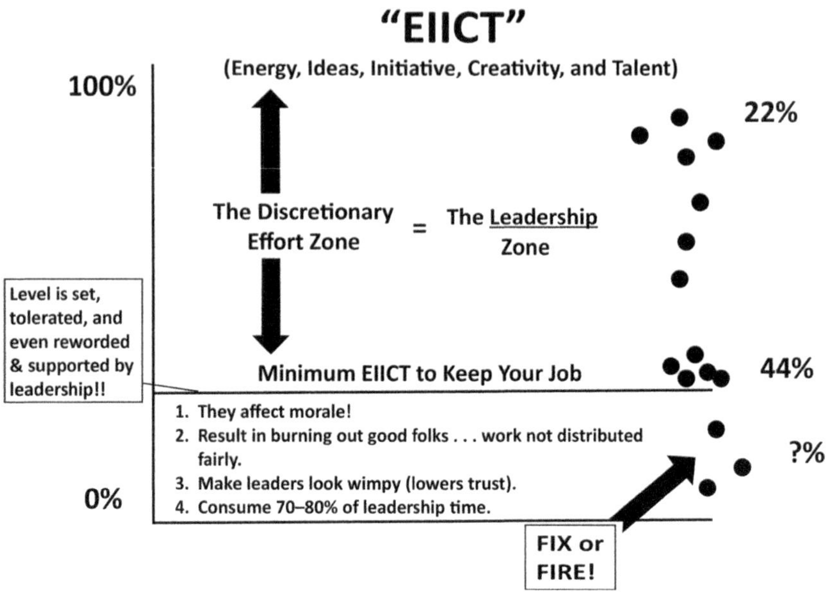

Let's examine this through the EIICT concept. This concept is the belief that people have several things or energies they can bring to any task at hand: energy, ideas, initiative, creativity and talent (EIICT). As shown in the diagram, people can bring anywhere from zero to nearly a hundred percent of their EIICT. (One example of bringing zero percent that I've heard was when an engineer in India did not show up to work for 24 years and continued to be paid the entire time!)

There is a line somewhere between zero and a hundred percent. This line is shown on my model and represents the minimum EIICT someone needs to bring to work without being fired. This line is set by what is allowed by management, fellow staff, lawyers, unions, and the culture itself. It varies from organization to organization.

I have consulted a fast-moving engineering company in California and for them, the line is set extremely high. In fact, when they offered a high-paying job to a candidate, they told him that he needed to bring in five times that salary in productivity. At the other end of the spectrum, I have been around government agencies where if you basically "have a pulse and can fog a mirror," they will keep you around until retirement. I consulted a government hospital and was astounded at how low the bar sometimes was and how poorly someone could perform and keep their job, even when it was impacting the health and safety of patients. While I am not anti-union, I have seen situations where unions make it almost impossible to fire someone who is not performing. This can be extremely frustrating for managers.

In one study by Gallup, 44 percent of respondents agreed that they did the minimum they needed to do to keep their jobs. Only 22 percent said they were working to their full potential. One other study in a business magazine several years ago suggested that, in average organizations, about 30 percent of people are "Bright Eyes," coming to work excited and hard charging. About 53 percent are "Glazed Eyes," basically hovering on or near the line. They come in and do their jobs, nothing more. Work has become, as I wrote previously, a day prison to them. They are admitted at eight and paroled at five, day after day. The remaining 17 percent are "Beady Eyes" and are doing what they can to oppose progress, hold others back, and create all kinds of stress, drama, and dysfunctionality.

Sadly, most people arrive the first day, week or even month on the job as Bright Eyes. But over time, they slowly gravitate downward, disillusioned, disempowered, and discouraged. They may end up on or even below the line.

This may seem a bit harsh, but if you notice on the EIICT diagram, there is a six month fix or fire box. I believe that if leaders and managers do everything mentioned in this book and are kind and try their best to correct a non-performer's behavior, they should let them go within no more than six months. It is evident that the person is unhappy and unmotivated in their job and is consciously or subconsciously "quitting and staying." In this case, it is better for all if they are allowed to move on and find value, meaning, and contribution somewhere else. This frees up their future. This was my experience when I found myself disenrolled and disengaged in the micromanaged culture of the university. I left to start my own company.

Firing someone is a last resort because sometimes their behavior can be corrected by assigning them to a brand-new position that better fits their talents and temperament. In essence, giving them a fresh start elsewhere in the company or team.

"Manage *to* the line. Lead *above* the line."

Traditional HR and management practices, such as counseling, "writing people up," and putting people on performance improvement plans, tend to keep people hovering above and below this minimum standard line. People fall below the line, administrative actions are taken, and they rise to the line for a while, and a few months later, they are below it again. Some then learn they can keep this up almost indefinitely. I call this narrow area the *Management Zone.*

To get people to rise to their highest potential, we need to get them to the *Leadership Zone* through inspiring leadership and applying leadership principles and tools, some of which I am outlining in this book. When we give people an inspiring vision, enroll them, and enable them, they can rise to great heights.

The bigger problem is those who consistently perform below the line (the Beady Eyes). In my experience, these people have at least four very negative impacts on the organization:

1. **They affect the morale of the top performers.** The Bright Eyes see these poor performers and feel almost violated. *"Why am I working this hard when I don't have to, and there is no recognition or value to me?"* They then consciously or subconsciously begin migrating down towards the Glazed Eye line.

2. **We burn out the Bright Eyes.** When people are underperforming, we take the work they should be doing and pile it on the top performers. Work begins to be distributed unfairly. Bright Eyes may start to see that and say, **"The harder I work, the more work they give me to do."** Suppose this added workload comes with little or no appreciation or recognition, or results in too much stress. In that case, they may either quit and leave, heading out to new opportunities, or worse yet, they quit and stay, joining the ranks of Glazed or even Beady Eyes.

3. **They make leaders look wimpy and lower trust in management.** Higher performing staff see the above two problems and wonder why management is not doing something about it. They think to themselves, *"If I were that person's manager, I would . . ."* This perceived lack of management action affects trust and people's belief that management can make tough decisions.

4. **We create stress in managers and waste leaders' time.** I often ask in my leadership workshops how much time and energy are eaten up by dealing with the problems and drama of the low performing Beady Eyes. Most tell me it is sixty to seventy percent of their time: time which could be devoted to releasing the full potential of other staff.

On a side note: I learned a couple of humorous acronyms for the Beady Eye poor performers:

- **CAVEmen/CAVEwomen:** Coworkers Against Virtually Everything. Those people habitually oppose anything new or different or anything proposed by management or other staff. Some even know they are this way and take pride in being "the Devil's Advocate."
- **BMW Club:** The Bitch, Moan, and Whine Club. Like CAVE, they whine and complain about everything. Sometimes, they can be difficult personalities. You find the BMW Club everywhere in life, not just at work.

Of course, there is a world of difference between those who are actively working against management and those who are merely frustrated.

When I discussed my Helm Model with a good friend who is working as a civilian employee for the Army in Germany, he made a powerful point. For disengaged and frustrated crew members, it is hard to look out of a porthole and see the ship heading for the rocks, knowing in their hearts it is going in the wrong direction but powerless to do anything but watch the looming danger. Sometimes, they even try to raise a warning cry but are told to return to their cubicles.

I heard an example of this many years ago in the early days of rocketry. A series of experimental rockets were launched only to have them explode prematurely. Leaders and engineers gathered around trying to figure out the problem. One of them left the room and went to the assembly line where the rockets were being built. He pulled aside one of the most experienced assemblers and said, "I bet you know what the problem is, don't you?"

The man said that he did. He held up a ring and said, "This is being put in backwards because that's what it says on the blueprint. If you let me turn it around, the rocket will fly."

The engineer asked him why he had not brought this up earlier. The assembler said that he had tried a couple of times but was dismissively told to mind his own business and go back to his job as an assembler.

Sometimes, if this happens to one crewmember who has his head figuratively "handed back to him on a plate," other crew members see this and keep their mouths shut. Just think what is lost!

So, How Do We Engage People?

People are engaged through the power of appreciation and recognition. Many books and treatises have addressed the ins and outs of human motivation for many centuries. I previously mentioned the excellent book *Drive: The Surprising Truth of What Motivates Us* by Daniel Pink. He debunks the traditional "carrots and sticks" theory of human motivation with detailed research that shows that the traditional HR offerings of more pay and better benefits don't have as much motivational power as giving people a compelling purpose, autonomy, and self-mastery. However, most people genuinely respond to recognition and rewards when they are applied skillfully.

Here are some examples of things I have experienced that motivated me, as well as some examples I have heard of in organizations.

Throughout my career in the Army, I received several formalized rewards, such as the Army Commendation Medal. These rewards were nice certificates enclosed in green folders with the Army logo on the outside. They were usually digitally signed by some upper-echelon leader that I didn't know or who didn't know me, along with a medal. To tell you the truth, I don't even know where those awards are today. I believe they are buried in a footlocker along with my old uniforms.

But there is one award that means a lot to me. In 1986, I was a company commander in the 7th Infantry Division at Fort Ord, California. The division commander was the most inspiring senior infantry leader I ever experienced firsthand. His name was Major General William H. Harrison. He had a tall and commanding presence, was an inspiring and motivating speaker, and led by example. Few people could keep up with him on division runs. He always started every address with his clear voice ringing out, "It's a great day to be in the Army, and it's a great day to be in the 7th Infantry Division in beautiful Fort Ord, California." We all smiled, knowing it was coming, and we believed it because we believed in him!

When he took command, he informed everyone that he was the only one allowed to write in purple ink, and everybody was to turn in any purple pens they had to the supply room. That way, when you saw something written in purple you know it came from the "Old Man" (a term usually affectionately applied to any top leader in the Army).

Every month, I was responsible for turning in a Unit Status Report (USR) for my command. This report detailed if my unit was ready for deployment in all major areas, such as personnel, equipment, and training. I dutifully sent the report forward, never thinking that it was read by the general himself (unless it contained very bad news!).

One morning, I was surprised and shocked when I came into my unit headquarters and found my first sergeant pointing to my desk. On my desk was an envelope addressed to my name in purple ink. With trembling hands, I opened it and took out my USR from the last month. On the top written in purple ink were the words, "Captain Miller/Kevin, you are a delight as a commander. God bless you, William H. Harrison." No Army award or recognition means as much to me as that simple note from a respected commander.

I have another personal example of the power of these simple actions. I had the joy in my life of knowing Dr. Stephen R. Covey, who became my friend and mentor. One time, I received this card in the mail. "Kevin—Thanks for all your good work. Keep blessing lives. I love and appreciate you, Stephen." That card stands where I can see it every day on the

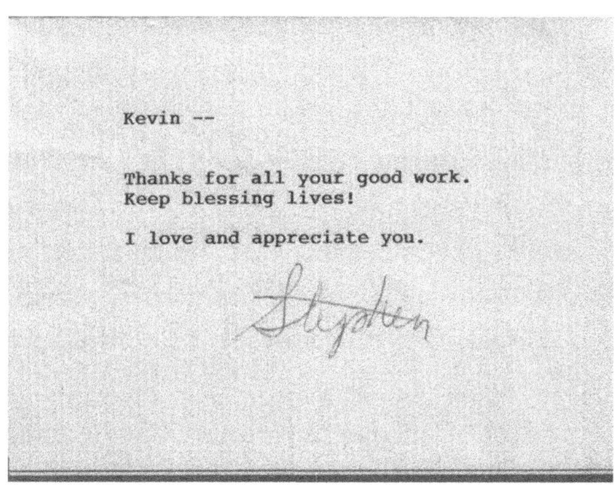

Kevin --

Thanks for all your good work.
Keep blessing lives!

I love and appreciate you.

Stephen

shelf above my computer. Sadly, he passed away in 2012, but sometimes I read it and say to myself, "I will do so, Stephen!"

These simple acts by senior leaders underscore the importance of giving personalized appreciation and recognition.

Many organizations think they are doing their job motivating and recognizing people with the Employee of the Month, Employee of the Quarter, and Employee of the Year awards with plaques on the wall. Research has proven these to have no bearing on how someone performs. No one gets up in the morning and says, "Well if I work hard today, I might be employee of the month!" Soon, employees figure out that if a person works or even breathes there long enough, they will end up on the wall, regardless of their performance, because it is their turn.

These kinds of programs do have their place, perhaps, and it is nice for an employee to have their moment in the sun and get the applause of their coworkers. But if you use them at all, they should be used only secondary to people receiving genuine, personalized recognition from leaders they trust.

I once attended a lecture by the HR vice president of a major hotel in Las Vegas. When he took over the hotel, he was shocked at the millions of dollars spent on costly housekeeping personnel turnover—almost two hundred percent per year. People stayed six months on average. Hiring and training this huge personnel turnover was very expensive.

He brought the housekeeping staff management together and asked what the problem was. Most of them immediately blamed the staff. "It's hard to get good people. These people don't want to work this hard, so they leave for greener pastures or a dollar an hour more."

The blame game went on for a half hour. As the VP listened to their blaming attitudes, he began to understand what the real problem might be—ineffective and demotivating team supervisors. He asked for a list of the last dozens of people who left and decided to call or visit them to interview them personally. The question he asked was simple, "Why did you leave working for us? Be honest."

After about twenty interviews, he felt sick to his stomach from the horror stories he heard about how they were treated by their managers and the negative culture of the housekeeping environment. One woman frankly said, "Well, I did throw the room lamp at my supervisor that day and walked out, but I didn't hit him!"

The VP asked, "Why?"

She said, "The human spirit can only take it so long."

"Take what?"

"We have about fifty things we have to do to clean up a room," she said. "We can do forty-nine things right, and nothing is ever said, but the supervisor comes around with a checklist, and finds the one thing we might have missed. They insultingly point it out to us. There was no way to win."

The VP decided to try a completely different approach: catch people doing something right. He had some poker chips engraved with a catchy recognition. They were made in four colors: red, white, blue, and gold. He brought the managers together and said, "From now on, we will look for the very best behaviors, the best work, and instantly recognize them with one of these chips."

The managers glumly indicated they thought it was a bad idea. So, he fired all of them on the spot! He told them they did not have the kind of leadership he needed.

The VP told us that he called the woman who threw the lamp and asked her if he could rehire her as a housekeeping manager, telling her he needed a new kind of positive leadership. She said, "I'll be there in fifteen minutes."

From that point on, managers went out of their way to find the very best room or bathroom or something else done extraordinarily well and gave out chips. The color determined how fantastic they thought the effort was. He then assigned a dollar value to the chips, which could be redeemed at the hotel gift shop.

The transformation that came from positive rewards and instant recognition was incredible. The VP told us that the turnover dropped to less than twenty percent the next year, and they have a waiting list of people wanting to work there. He was most surprised that people rarely redeemed the chips—the simple token of appreciation meant more to them as they shared and talked with each other. He said, "Recently, I heard a 'jingle-jingle' coming down the hall. One of the housekeepers had drilled all the chips she had received and hung them on small suction cups on the side of her cleaning cart. The noise reminded her of the joy of her success."

He ended by telling us that this program had saved the hotel over four million dollars a year, and the cleanliness of the hotel had never been better.

Another example came from a tour I made around a client's departments. I noticed Raisinette candy packages tacked on people's cubicle walls. He told me that when a staff member did something truly outstanding, he would say to them, "If I could, I would give you a raise—but I can give you my Raisinette award!"

The people loved and sought this recognition and would eat the candy but tack the package where they and others could see it. That way, they could instantly remember what they had done to earn it.

Another manager told me he did the same thing with Kudo bars—representing a kudo he thought a staff member deserved. The point here is simple: it doesn't take much, and it doesn't cost much. It just takes leaders who look for the good in people and extend almost instant and sincere recognition for specific things they see going well.

My final advice is to get everyone involved in recognizing the good in each other. One creative way I saw was a traveling trophy. It was an empty Spam can mounted on a trophy base. The team told me that Spam stood for "Super Positive Attitude Master," and they passed the trophy around each week. Whoever received the trophy one week was then looking for someone to give it to the next week in a staff meeting. The new recipient would keep it on their desk for the week. This took the responsibility away from the manager to do all the recognition. Once someone had received the trophy, they went to the manager's office for a dark blue T-shirt with the image of a Spam can on the front and the words "Super Positive Attitude Master" on the back. They could wear this shirt all day on the last Friday of the month.

Other creative examples I have seen or heard of include:

- One boss makes gourmet sack lunches and leaves them on someone's desk with a note of appreciation.
- Another manager brings soap and water and washes an employee's car for them during work and leaves a note on their windshield.

- In the early days of Microsoft, Bill Gates would come in late at night and sit down with staff members in the all-night dining and break room, asking them about their work and thanking them.

Most people are emotionally starving for positive expressions of appreciation and recognition. This is true for any generation, but research shows it is particularly true for the younger workforce—many grow up accustomed to instant recognition and reinforcement from video games! It is hard for them to enter an environment where only mistakes are noticed, and most feedback is negative.

If you want other ideas on providing recognition and motivation, I recommend Bob Nelson's great books *1001 Ways to Energize Employees* and *1001 Ways to Motivate Employees.*

The Power of Delegating

One of the most powerful tools for engaging people is learning to delegate properly. Delegation allows you to distribute challenges, opportunities, and tasks fairly across the workforce. It allows you to help people develop. It enables senior leaders to focus their time and energy on things that are their responsibility. It energizes and integrates the workforce. It helps create a spirit of ownership.

So, what should you delegate? Typically, it's important to delegate the routine tasks that need to be done. However, it is also important to delegate challenging non-routine tasks (perhaps using the 200 Talent sheet downloadable on our website). Delegate things that will help people stretch, develop, and expand their boundaries. It shows them that you trust them. (Keep in mind that they may need a little more guidance as you develop them.)

There are several reasons why leaders, including parents, do not delegate. One common one is that it may take longer to have someone else do something than to do it yourself! You can pick up a child's room in five minutes, but it will take them half an hour (and maybe your time and energy nagging) to do it! That may be a valid reason in the short term, but it does nothing to develop capabilities in the future.

I once heard a great quote: "If you routinely do something for someone something they can do for themselves, you ultimately disempower them. The key here is *routinely*. If you routinely do for an employee or a child or youth something that they could learn to do for themselves, you will weaken them and make them dependent upon you to do the thinking and action. Conveniently, they may also have you to blame if it does not turn out!"

(Of course, this does not mean we can't routinely do nice things for others or our team!)

Here are several steps to keep in mind to delegate effectively. You can also download a form or worksheet from the tools section of our website.

1. First, choose the right person, keeping in mind what I mentioned above. Resist the temptation to always go to your go-to person. Sometimes, we find Pareto's Rule applying at work: 20% of the people do 80% of the work. This frustrates the high performers and causes burnout. It denies growth opportunities for others.

2. Next, explain to them why the task is important, how it affects the mission, and why you specifically chose them. Enroll them in the purpose and importance of the task and outcome! You might even refer to the vision and mission and explain why this task is aligned with one of the major objectives.

3. Now, describe in general but clear terms the framework of the assignment so they have a clear image in their mind of what the framework is and what the outcome should generally look like.

Resist offering any specific instructions at this point even if they ask. If you do, they will likely take these ideas as directives, and it will limit their creativity and ownership.

4. Now, ask them for their initial ideas for how they could proceed. Ask them if they have any questions. Again, resist jumping in even if they stall out for a moment without any ideas. Express your confidence in them that they will come up with something great and perhaps suggest resources they might research or turn to.

5. Be sure to let them know the degree of initiative that they should take with this assignment. Note that different steps of the project or assignment could have different degrees of initiative. Here are the five degrees of initiative:

a. Level Five (the highest): Take whatever action you choose and report back to me in our routine meeting.
b. Level Four: Take whatever action you choose, but report back to me immediately. This is because the action is perhaps timely or sensitive, and the manager needs to be aware of what was done.
c. Level Three: Come up with recommendations and bring them to me so we can decide which is best. Here, the manager reserves the decision-making.
d. Level Two: Ask me what to do. The manager gives the person a heads-up about what is coming, and the person may periodically ask what they can do to help.
e. Level One: Wait until told. Do nothing and wait for guidance.

We want as many things as possible to be Levels Five or Four, but it requires high trust in the person's capability to make their own decisions and act. There may be more than one step in the delegation: it may start as Level Three but then move to Four and Five once the action has been decided.

6. Let them know any deadlines, how often, and how you want them to report back to you.

7. At the end, you can ask them if they have any questions, but, again, be sure to leave most of the thinking and initiative in their hands. Otherwise, you may turn them into a simple "go-fer." Have the person repeat to you exactly what they understood regarding the desired outcome, any constraints and limitations, and what degree of initiative they have.

You may find that some people initially resist you giving them so much autonomy and self-direction. They may be afraid of this freedom and prefer you tell them what to do. If you do, you become responsible for the outcome, and they cannot be held accountable. Also, it is hard for them to feel the joy of achievement and self-growth because they only did what you told them to do. Stephen R. Covey wisely said, "You cannot hold people accountable for results if you continue to supervise their methods."

Green and Clean: This is one of my favorite stories from the home life of Stephen R. Covey. The best way to learn this right now is to see him tell it himself by searching "green and clean" on YouTube. But let me summarize.

Stephen Covey delegated to one of his sons the responsibility of caring for the yard. He gave the young man a very clear vision of what good would look like each week: green and clean! He pointed to his neighbor's yard, which was always green and clean, and said, "That's the color we're after!"

When the boy asked him how to do it, Stephen said, "Well, you can use buckets or a hose or spit all day long just as long as the outcome is green and clean."

Because the boy was quite young, Stephen worked alongside him to show him how to do it. Stephen offered himself as one of the resources, and the son could ask for help at any time.

As the story progresses, the boy begins to fail in his assignment. Day after day, the grass was turning brown, and clutter and trash started building up on the lawn. They had agreed that they would walk around the yard once a week and see how it was going. The boy turned to tears and cried out, "It's so hard!"

What was so hard? He had done nothing! Covey points out that what is hard is moving up the level of initiative. Rather than getting angry, he said, "Our agreement was that you could ask me for help. Can I help you right now?"

The boy eagerly said yes, and they worked together. From that moment on, he only asked for help once or twice during the summer. (As a caveat, the son, Stephen M. R. Covey, has a different perspective on the event, which you can see on YouTube!)

The lesson here is clear: when you delegate something, try to make sure that the person understands exactly and clearly what the desired end state will look like. Give the maximum leeway to achieve that objective in any way they wish. There may be some upfront limitations in time, money, and regulations, so be sure those are clearly understood.

I once took this principle to a group of people, and a woman came up to me months later and told me about a brilliant way in which she applied this to her children cleaning up their rooms. She soon found that her standard of cleanliness was much different than theirs was! She would tell them to clean up their room, and they would come out five minutes later. She would go in and find they had basically kicked everything under the bed! She realized they had no idea what the standard visually looked like. So, she took time to work with each child, having fun getting their room "green and clean"—bringing it to a perfect standard. She then helped them see and feel how nice it felt and how useful it was to have all their toys organized and things clean and neat. They enjoyed a special treat together in the newly minted room.

But she realized she had to capture this picture in time. So, she pulled out her digital camera and took photographs of the room in its perfect state, including the inside closet and made-up bed (even under the bed!).

She printed these pictures and put them on a poster inside their bedroom door with the words "clean room." She then established the rule and the reward. She said, "I will come around at noon on Saturday and compare your room to the pictures on the poster. If your room looks like the poster, I will put your allowance in an envelope on the bed. If it does not, I will keep your allowance in my personal Mom's own 'fun fund' to spend on myself. And I will give you two extra hours of special labor during the week, like cleaning the garage, weeding, or washing the car. But it is entirely up to you because I will never nag you." And she never does. Each child knows and even sees the standards and the rules and consequences, and it is up to them to live them or not.

She told me it is cute to watch her five-year-old girl clean her room, look at the poster, move a stuffed animal two inches to the right on her dresser, and peer under the bed to make sure there was nothing there. But her greatest victory occurred near noon one Saturday when her 13-year-old daughter was cleaning her 15-year-old brothers' room for him according to the standard on the poster. She asked her daughter why she was doing it, and the girl said that her brother had called from Scout camp that morning and promised her that if she cleaned his room, she could have half his allowance! It worked so well that the mother applied it to other things like the dish job—taking pictures of what a correctly loaded dishwasher and clean sink look like.

These are examples of creating win-win agreements. In the case of clean rooms, everyone can win. One father set a win-win agreement with his son as he was turning 16 and anxious to drive. In the written signed agreement, the son's win was that dad would pay for the car insurance, maintenance, and most of the gas, and the boy could use the car anytime it was free and for legitimate, legal reasons. In return, the parents' win was that the boy would drive or run errands whenever they needed him if he was available, not doing homework or non-recreational things. The boy would wash and vacuum the car every weekend and contribute five dollars a week toward gas. Of course, the 16-year-old was initially eager to drive anytime! There were written consequences if the agreement was violated. A win all the way around. Of course, the boy's excitement at being able to drive soon waned a bit, but if he resisted a request to drive his sibling or go to the store, the agreement and consequences stood.

In all these cases, we are releasing and engaging the potential of people. They are learning, growing, and developing. They can contribute meaningfully to the vision and purpose and feel the joy of self-accomplishment.

One of the best ways to engage people is to use them in their talents. It is entirely possible for you to work with someone for years and not know that they are a talented pianist or party planner! I mentioned the 200 Talents available for download in the tool section of our website. Distribute the tool to everyone and ask them to circle all the items on the list where they feel they have some talent and interest. Keep a copy for yourself and give one to them. When something comes up that could be assigned or delegated, you might look at the 200 Talents lists and find the right person for the task. An example might be planning the office Christmas party. (Notice that one of the items on the list is "party planner"!) The right person for the job might be the newest person on the team or someone who has never been given a significant assignment.

I was at one time a consultant to a large university library. A manager told me that he had an extremely disengaged student employee assigned to return books to their shelves. She was miserably and robotically doing the job. We had her take the 200 Talents, and she circled everything artistic! So, he was having a right-brained artist doing a very mechanical left-brain task.

The manager had a problem with students coming dressed improperly to work because they had a higher standard of dress in the library. He pulled her aside and asked if she could create a series of posters to remind students about the dress code. He handed her the department charge card to go purchase materials, and she practically ran out of the office. He told her she could work on the posters during work time but would like them in a week.

He was surprised to have her standing at the door the next morning with the posters already artistically done. She told him she had rushed home and worked on them all evening because she couldn't wait! He had her introduce the posters to the applause of her fellow students. From that moment on, she was one of the most engaged students on his team, and a year later, he assigned her to be the student team lead.

You can delegate authority, but you can never delegate responsibility after delegating a task to someone else. If you picked the right person, fine; but if you picked the wrong man, the responsibility is yours—not his. —Richard E. Krafve

---

What Richard E. Krafve means is that we, as leaders, cannot wash our hands of the ultimate responsibility for what we have delegated to others. We can assign accountability but never totally relinquish responsibility.

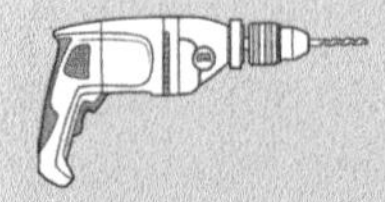

Application Ideas

1. Think about your team through the EIICT concept: Who are your top performers? Who is "riding the line" doing the bare minimum, and who is below the line? Seek to deeply understand where people are and what is needed to help motivate and develop them.

2. Create action teams to brainstorm ideas on how to engage people at work better.

3. In your family, look for new ways to enable everyone to engage in the work of the home. Have a family brainstorming session to work out ideas.

4. Devise a clever way for people to visually see what the final standard is, like the clean room example.

5. Watch my video on delegating on www.VisionBound.com or on the VisionBound YouTube channel.

CHAPTER NINE

Exploring New Horizons

Who can forget the opening of many episodes of Star Trek, where Captain James T. Kirk says, "Space: the final frontier. These are the voyages of the starship Enterprise. Its five-year mission: to explore strange new worlds, to seek out new life and new civilizations, to boldly go where no one has gone before!"

I witnessed a perfect example of courageously leaving the secure and unknown to venture into a new business field. About ten years ago, my wife and I were traveling through beautiful country roads outside Danville, Ohio. We were charmed by the Amish furniture stores along the way and passed several of them until something prompted me to turn into one of them.

We were greeted by a wonderful Amish gentleman, Raymond Weaver, who was dressed in traditional Amish clothing in his very rustic store. We engaged in conversation about business, and I found he was an avid fan of my friend, Stephen R. Covey. To make a long story short, Raymond and his family had the courage to change religions and start an entirely new life. They expanded their business, learned to drive, get more electricity, and made many life and business changes. Their family, Amish friends, and business associates completely shunned them for this decision. Raymond's own father and mother disowned them, and former friends and buyers turned their backs on them. They started home-schooling when the local school would not enroll their children. In short, they lost everything because of a new-found faith and vision. They had to start almost completely over.

In the years since, Raymond and Laura have forged new paths, expanded their attractive furniture and farm/petting zoo, and opened their wonderful pretzel business in a Walmart store this past year. Each time I talk to Raymond or visit his farm at weaversfarmandfurniture.com, his eyes sparkle with more creative ideas. He gained much more than he lost by boldly going!

For many years, I had a quote on my wall, *"A man cannot hope to discover new oceans until he has courage to lose sight of the shore."*

The next part of our Helm Model is very crucial. Leaders know that nothing is perfect and that all systems can be improved. This does not mean to engage in "change for change's sake." People resist "flavor of the month" initiatives. It means that we are constantly benchmarking and stretching to find new and better ways to do business and serve customers.

An example of bold exploration happened in the 1970s when Sony released the Walkman. Before then, no customer had requested that Sony create a personal portable audio device they could wear on their belt that could play cassette tapes and radio stations. The reason is simple: no customer thought such a thing was possible! But Sony engineers, led by Sony founders Masaru Ibuka and Akio Morita, brainstormed and created the Walkman. It was released to the market in 1979. It became an instant success, and Sony had to open many new factories to keep up with the demand. Competitors were caught shorthanded and soon were creating their own versions. But from that point on, the product was called a "Walkman," no matter who manufactured it. Sony got there first because they explored. And Sony created its own future.

Sometimes companies get to market with a product so soon and so skillfully that the product's brand becomes the generic name for the product line itself. Few people in a store ask where the facial tissue is—they ask for Kleenex. It's the same with Band-Aids.

A great book called *Blue Ocean Strategy: How to Create Uncontested Market Space and Make the Competition Irrelevant* by W. Chan Kim presents many ideas on how to explore "boldly going where no one has gone before" in your market. This is, in essence, what Sony did. This kind of exploration will take most everyone's thinking on your team. And you must think creatively and "love it for a minute" when new and even far-out ideas come forth.

Another interesting idea is found in the book, *If it Ain't Broke . . . Break it!* by Robert Kriegel. He dares all of us to leave the conventional business ideas behind and dare to break them to create new vistas.

One example I heard when I was in Alaska. At the time, they faced a rather unique problem: ice storms would build up ice on powerlines in remote areas, causing them to break. Sending teams on snowmobiles was dangerous, time-consuming, and expensive. So, they came together and had a brainstorming session.

As they brainstormed, one rather new staff member said, "There are a lot of bears in Alaska. Maybe we could use them to climb the power poles and knock off the ice." (Imagine a lot of electrocuted bears falling to the ground!)

Instead of laughing, the manager ran with it and said, "Interesting idea, but how would we get the bears to climb the poles?"

The staff member thought for a moment, then said, "Bears like honey, so we could put pots of honey on top of the poles to get them to climb."

The manager asked how they would get the honey pots to the top of the poles. The staff member's answer was simple: by helicopter.

The manager said, "What would be the problem with that?"

"The prop wash from the blades would blow the pots off," the staff member answered. Then, they both almost simultaneously got it—the prop wash would also blow the ice off!

So now, according to the story I was told, they use helicopters to fly low along the powerlines and blow the ice off, essentially using the choppers as giant fans! This idea would never have come to them had they not asked searching questions and thought outside of the box. It took a great leader to keep probing. The staff member was given a large bonus, and the state saved hundreds of thousands of dollars.

Great explorers need to abandon their self-imposed paradigms. The word *paradigm* comes from the Greek word *paradeigma*, which means "the pattern we expect to see." We all have paradigms formed over a lifetime of observations, social and family programming, and life experiences. We are hardly aware of them until, like a fish taken from the water, we are forced to see things differently.

A tragic example of a short-sighted paradigm happened with the Swiss watchmaking industry. For centuries, the Swiss prided themselves on being the creators of beautiful, intricate gear-driven watches and clocks. No one could match their quality and reputation. Their paradigm was that "we are watchmakers," not "we are the world's timekeepers."

This paradigm kept them locked in the past, with disaster looming. In the early 1960s, some of their engineers were experimenting and found that a small electrical current passing through a quartz crystal created vibrations that were more accurate measures of time. They saw this discovery as a mere curiosity. They went on to put it out on display at a watchmaker convention in Zürich *with no patent!*

Guess who stood around looking at it? Engineers from a small company called Timex. Within a few years, Seiko, Timex, and other competitors flooded the market with inexpensive watches that did not require winding and kept better time. According to several estimates, the number of Swiss watch companies dropped from over 1,600 in 1970 to fewer than 600 by the mid-1980s, and the number of employees plummeted from 90,000 in 1970 to 33,000 in 1984.

To some degree, every individual and organization has paradigms, many of which go unnoticed and unquestioned and drive down their ability to be creative. At the same time, we must preserve the core values and products that make us great. Perhaps this can be illustrated by the ancient yin and yang symbol.

Preserving the core comes when we recognize the products, values, and processes that have made us successful. But sometimes, we also must get rid of our time-honored traditions.

Coca-Cola was introduced to the world in 1889 and is now the most universally recognized brand in the world with its unique font on a bright red background.

But Coca-Cola's paradigm does not limit itself to one color. My wife Denise and I were traveling up the Amazon River. We came to Parintins, whose inhabitants are sharply divided in their allegiance to two different soccer teams. (In Brazil, soccer borders on a national religion!) One team wears red jerseys, and one wears blue. The fanaticism is so intense that many people paint their front door red or blue to know who they can be friends with!

It became clear that no blue team member or fan would ever hold a red Coke can at a ball game. So, Coca-Cola responded. Now, when you go to a grocery store in that city, the red Coke cans are on one side of the store, and the blue Coke cans are on the other. I bought one as a souvenir of a company willing to explore and challenge the past to create the future.

But even experienced companies make mistakes and assumptions. One that comes to mind is the disaster Coca-Cola faced when introducing the New Coke formula on April 23, 1985. They sweetened their original formula to match more closely that of Pepsi, which had successfully launched major ad campaigns with supposed taste tests starring Michael Jackson. Coca-Cola turned its back on the classic recipe it introduced in 1886 (which contained cocaine that was removed in 1903!). The decision wasn't made to be more like Pepsi. It had more to do with cutting costs by eliminating some of the more expensive ingredients in the original formula.

Consumers revolted, and loyalty was lost. It cost Coca-Cola millions of dollars to correct the problem. They rebranded the original Coke as Coke Classic and finally eliminated the new Coke formula in 2002. This blunder is a classic study in business school today. Still, New Coke was somewhat successful because it created a big news story, revitalized the brand, and renewed public attraction to Coke.

A much more recent example happened when, in April 2023, Bud Light created a marketing plan using a transgender social media influencer. They failed to gauge the strong negative reaction from hundreds of thousands of their core customers. This debacle cost Anheuser-Busch hundreds of millions of dollars, and other light beer brands, such as Modelo, unseated Bud Light as the leading light beer in the market. Despite many attempts to back-track the image, sales have not recovered as of early 2024.

A final thought before moving to brainstorming: As we explore and create new ideas, it is good to keep in mind a great quote by General George S. Patton: "A good plan violently executed right now is far better than a perfect plan executed next week." There comes a golden moment when it is time to act now and to "adjust fire" later.

I learned this watching an artillery demonstration at Fort Lewis, Washington. The target for the gunners was a burned-out hulk of an old vehicle downrange. A helicopter flew in and sling-loaded a 105 MM howitzer out to the ground, followed by an artillery crew who rappelled down to the gun. The gunnery sergeant put his binoculars to his eyes and made his best guess of where the first round should hit. He did not expect it to strike. He used it as a TRP (target reference point) and quickly gave the second order, deliberately "bracketing" the target. Now, with those two points, he said, "Right three, down two, fire for effect." The third round hit the target dead on. Impressively, all of this took only fifteen seconds. Now, if he had had only one round, he would have had to take more time to calculate to hit the target dead on.

There are times when we need to move quickly, or a competitor or other factors will fire first. Quickly getting "steel down range" gets things moving, creates momentum and energizes the team. Brainstorming is a time-honored method to get many creative solutions on the table, and then you can "fire for effect" on the best one.

How to Brainstorm

So, how do we avoid the pitfalls of paradigms limiting our ability to explore and create a new future? Try this simple process for brainstorming.

1. Bring your team together and list all the things you would like to explore. These can be new products, processes, or significant problems that need to be solved.

Choose one of these as the "issue of the week" and post it on a flip chart where everyone can see and think creatively about it all week long. Then, bring together a group of diverse and creative people and follow this process:

Put some flip chart paper on the wall, go around the room person by person, and ask them to submit one idea on the issue. Do not evaluate or judge and write down the idea just as it is said.

Spin around the room person by person, and if someone does not have an idea, they can simply say "pass." You may find that one somewhat crazy idea spurs someone else's thinking, and the list can become very creative.

2. When it seems that most ideas have been exhausted, combine similar ideas and make a new list. Be sure not to allow anyone to dominate.

3. Begin the evaluation process. Look at each idea and evaluate its feasibility. Maybe it is feasible later but not now, or maybe it is completely out of any realm of possibility.

At this point, I recommend applying the simple advice to "love it for a minute." Rather than immediately dismissing the idea, everyone agrees to "love it for a minute." Look at the idea from all sides to see if there might be some great value in it. This prevents preconceived paradigms and attitudes from immediately discounting something. This is such a powerful concept that it might be part of your team's code of conduct: "We love it for a minute."

As you evaluate, you gradually narrow things down to one or two very creative and forward-thinking ideas. At this point, you may organize task forces and assign the ideas to them for further development. Don't dismiss the group until you know who does what, when it needs to be done by, and how the follow-up will go.

This process includes much diversity and experience, longevity, age, and gender. I read a statistic once that said about 60% of the ideas that truly revolutionize businesses come from employees who have been there less than six months. They have not been there long enough to be hardened in their thinking and thus see things with a fresh eye.

As a consultant, or when leading brainstorming sessions myself for a client, I sometimes tell them upfront that I am the symbolic "village know-nothing" in the room. Sometimes, the curious person asks the obvious questions that others cannot see and questions the status quo.

You also need a mixture of thinking styles. The right brain left brain concept has been around for many years and has somewhat been diluted as brain researchers find many variations of how people think.

Regardless, it is still essential to bring together individuals with different thinking styles. Some may be more logical, and others may be more creative and artistic, and together, they will create a more complex and complete view of an issue.

Many new studies also show differences between male and female brain design. One major study by Cambridge University shows that there are over 100 physiological differences between a male brain and a female brain, and this accounts for how men and women communicate, relate, and approach problems from different angles. As a consultant, I would much rather work with a team of both men and women than a team of all men or all women for that reason. I present more of this information on gender differences in Tool Number Seven in the Toolbox section. The same applies to age differences and generational differences.

No matter how intelligent and educated we are, we cannot begin to truly foresee the future. When I was born in 1954, Scientific American magazine printed a photo of how scientists at the Rand Corporation envisioned what a home computer would look like in 50 years. It was the size of a wall and even had a steering wheel! The caption in the photo indicated it was not a working model. But "with teletype interface and the Fortran language," the computer would be relatively easy to use! (I learned to program with Fortran in 1974!)

We laugh today thinking that those great engineers would think Fortran would still be the language programming tool in 50 years. But how could they imagine having a mobile smartphone in a pocket and a car in our garage today, both with more computing power than the Apollo spacecraft that took astronauts to the moon in 1969?

We need to challenge our paradigms, think way outside the box, and be willing to challenge the status quo. As Albert Einstein said,

"The significant problems we face in the world today will not be solved at the same level of thinking that created them."

I am also intrigued by the photograph of a young Steve Jobs and Steve Wozniak displaying their initial ideas for a home computer at a large computer trade show in the 1970's. Most people walking by gave them a condescending smile and walked on. One senior executive and top engineer from a major computer company said, "Who would possibly want a computer in their home?"

So, Steve Jobs went on to create his own company and the rest is history. He did it again when he released the first iPhone on January 9th, 2007. In an amazingly short time, it put BlackBerry out of business. (A great movie, *BlackBerry* portrays this compelling story.)

It is essential that we recognize and reward creativity from wherever it comes. I was once consulting a senior executive and noticed a brass plate on his door which read "Problems are welcome as long as you bring at least one well-thought-out solution." He absolutely enforces this rule. No one can bring a problem to him unless they have thought of a solution. He said, "I do not want a bunch of golden retrievers fetching problems and eagerly bringing them to me. I need creative thinkers."

In their book *Sacred Cows Make the Best Burgers*, Robert J. Kriegel and David Brandt share many examples of the progress often made by challenging the "sacred cows" long held by organizations. One of my favorite examples came from a prominent tire company. They spent millions wrapping tires with protective paper. One teenager, who was hired for the summer, questioned why the paper was needed. He was told that the paper was there to protect the whitewall tires. What whitewall tires? Those had fallen to the wayside years ago, having been popular in the 1950's and 60's. But even though the company no longer sold those tires, they continued needlessly wrapping all of their tires with paper. The teenager's observation led to them eliminating the process and saving the company about five million dollars a year. They rewarded the boy with a nice bonus.

For more information about creative thinking, I recommend the book *First Break all the Rules: What the World's Greatest Managers Do Differently* by Don Clifton. I also recommend learning more about a concept called the Six Thinking Hats that was introduced in 1985 by Edward de Bono in his book by that title. This concept involves creating six different colors of ball caps, literally or figuratively. Each color represents a type of thinking and role the wearer plays in the brainstorm. The colors are as follows:

- Blue: The Big Picture
- Red: Feelings and Emotions
- White: Facts and Information
- Black: Critical Judgement
- Yellow: Positive
- Green: New Ideas

The roles above show how a problem can be approached in a very balanced way as each person plays their role. Green might introduce a new idea, and yellow brings out the positives in the concept. White introduces facts and information to support or challenge the idea. Black balances with some critical judgment about why it may or may not work or something the group is not thinking about. Red brings in the feelings others might have about it and does an ego check. Blue ensures that the big picture is kept in mind, so the group does not get lost in the weeds.

I have used this process with different groups and found it extremely useful in preventing the dreaded groupthink problem, where people quickly jump on the bandwagon or blindly follow the bosses' lead. It helps ensure a balanced approach to the problem or issue.

Imagination is more important than knowledge. —Albert Einstein

---

Exploring the Future in Customer Service

Exploring the future in customer service has become increasingly critical in recent years. It is now almost impossible to rely on products or price differentiation alone to carve a niche in the market. As soon as a good idea or product is released, competitors soon mirror it. And someone, somewhere, will sell it cheaper or faster, if only on Amazon or E-bay! The way to truly differentiate is first having the right people, then top-notch service policies, procedures, and strategies. To do this, challenge every process, every procedure, and every policy to see if there is a better way to do it from the customer's standpoint.

I have witnessed that, over time, organizations tend to organize and create procedures and policies that make work easier or more efficient from the employees' standpoint. Managers also tend to have a knee-jerk reaction and write policies to cover every unusual situation that arises, not recognizing that they have created an extra step or frustration for 99% of their employees. Soon, policy and procedures manuals are inches thick, and customer's frustrations are a mile high. Some organizations and leaders punish the 99 for the mistakes of the one, meaning when one staff member does something amiss, they create a policy that constrains and punishes everyone.

A great religious leader was asked over a century ago how he successfully governed a disparate group of converts from a dozen nations. He simply said, "I teach them correct principles, and they govern themselves." We can follow this creed in our own leadership at home and at work: challenge the process, reduce as much as possible into clear principles, and release employees to govern themselves accordingly.

To challenge and explore all operations successfully, I suggest the following:

1. Constantly examine the operation from different viewpoints. Ask all staff, customers, and users what is frustrating or less helpful to them.

2. Reward problem-*solving*, not problem-*finding*. Challenge others to not bring a problem without at least two possible solutions and a recommendation of which one is best.

3. Engage in frequent brain-storming sessions, as outlined earlier in the chapter.

4. Shop the competition and do research to benchmark what the very best are doing. Never get complacent.

5. Be flexible to meet the changing market and societal demands. Keep an eye on social trends and try to be ahead of the curve.

6. The best way to predict the future is to *create* it. Find a product or service strategy that no one else has thought of. Remember the Sony Walkman? Time Magazine lists it as one of the most influential gadgets and gismos. Soon, dozens of manufacturers made similar devices, but customers still asked for a Walkman. What is the equivalent of the Sony Walkman in your market today? Don't wait for customers to ask for it: build it, and they will come!

7. Listen to customers and staff. Hold focus groups like Sony does. Involve all stakeholders in challenging your processes. First-line service staff often are the ones that know what systems most frustrate customers or internal staff and what products or services are in demand.

In summary, this chapter covers the basics of exploring: finding new and better ways to do just about anything and trying to be innovative. We now have covered the five spokes of the Helm model by envisioning, enrolling, enabling, engaging, and exploring. But what happens if the very center axis, the hub, breaks or falls off? This is where trust comes in.

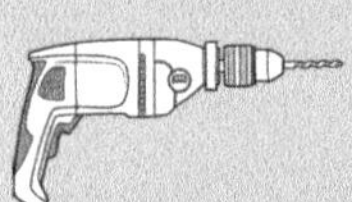

Now, it is time to go to work with these new power tools.

1. Follow the brainstorming process by making a list of the problems you most want to solve. Lead your team through the brainstorming steps. You can even do this in your family and include your children.
2. Challenge the limitations of your own thinking and paradigms.

CHAPTER TEN

The Axis of Trust

We turn now to perhaps the most important part of our Helm Model. Without trust in the center axis, nothing can move effectively. In our model, if the axis of trust breaks, the wheel falls off!

2,500 years ago, Socrates said, "The beginning of wisdom is the definition of terms." How do we define *trust* as a noun and trust as a verb?

The following definitions are from Dictionary.com:

> **noun**
>
> reliance on the integrity, strength, ability, surety, etc., of a person or thing; confidence
>
> confident expectation of something; hope

verb (used without object)

to rely upon or place confidence in someone or something

to have confidence; hope: *Things work out if one only trusts.*

These powerful words stand out to me from those definitions: reliance, integrity, ability, confidence, and hope.

Back to our helm, imagine what can happen if the axis breaks, if the wheel gets rusty and is unable to turn. And thus, it is with trust. When trust breaks down or is lost, everything can go with it. That is why it's at the very center of our Helm Model.

I am sure you have seen this happen in life situations. Companies collapse or even go bankrupt almost overnight when terrible violations of trust or ethics violations occur (Enron). Prominent leaders and sports figures nearly dissolve from the public view due to ethics or moral violations (Mike Tyson). Political figures nearly destroy the economies and functionality of their countries (Idi Amin in Uganda).

We earn trust with others when we show both integrity and competence. Let me illustrate with a personal experience.

I was a company commander in the 7th Infantry Division when I led my company through an intensive Light Fighter's Course at Fort Ord, California. On the first day, I led my group to a confidence and course building exercise. The exercise required us to crawl through lanes while a machine gun, firing live ammunition, fired less than ten inches over our heads. I led the way, as leaders should. As I crawled along the lane, hearing the searing whiz of bullets singing over my head, I realized how much trust and confidence I had in at least three things: 1) the skill of the gunner, 2) the security of the logs forming the sides of the lane, and the maintenance systems that ensured the machine gun was operating safely and would only shoot where it was meant to go! Luckily, all of us made it through. Similar experiences apply to paratroopers jumping out of a plane.

Recently, in Utah, trusting citizens were bilked out of millions of dollars by an untrustworthy but prominent person in a Ponzi scheme. They were promised a huge return on investment through gold and silver. Instead, the unscrupulous manager of the scheme used the money to buy expensive mansions, automobiles, and sexual services.

In this case, the *person* was untrustworthy, and the *system* itself was illegal and faulty, designed as an elaborate way to steal from trusting investors. According to data published by the Federal Trade Commission (FTC), consumers reported losing approximately $8.8 billion to fraud in 2022, with investment scams making up more than $3.8 billion. This data published by the FTC indicates consumers lost 30% more due to fraud in 2022 than in 2021.

The sad thing is that many of these victims are trusting seniors hoping to leave a financial legacy for their families.

One outstanding book on trust is *The Speed of Trust* by Stephen M. R. Covey. The subtitle on the book cover claims trust is the *one* thing that changes *everything*. In high-trust cultures, everything moves faster and costs less. In low-trust cultures, everything slows down and costs more.

These costs aren't just monetary. Low trust costs a lot in terms of engagement, productivity, and commitment.

A simple analogy is that of a bank account. With a normal bank account, we make deposits and withdrawals to keep our financial life moving. But each of us also have an emotional bank account or EBA with nearly every significant relationship in our lives. This EBA also could be called a trust account or a TA. As we do the good things that we have discussed in this book and other caring and loving things, we are making constant deposits to these emotional bank accounts and trust accounts. Each time we do something that violates the principles of good leadership or healthy relationships, we can take withdrawals from these accounts.

Sometimes, this can be done almost subconsciously without us even being aware of it, especially if we are not in tune with what the other person values (whether something is a deposit or a withdrawal is determined by the person, not by you). These negative withdrawals can be slow and incremental, like tiny leaks from a bucket.

Sadly, a major violation of trust can drain the entire account in an instant, such as with the above-mentioned investment scams.

Because we are human, we will make these withdrawing mistakes, and no one can go through their life without making withdrawals from trust accounts and emotional accounts, even with the people they love and value the most. Therefore, it becomes even more important for us to fill the bucket consciously and continuously with regular acts of kindness, recognition, appreciation, and many of the things that we have presented in this book. When we envision, enroll, enable, engage, and explore with others, these can become great deposits in trust accounts.

This analogy does not just apply to individuals but to entire organizations. Every organization earns a level of trust with its clients. in the marketplace, and even in society. Usually, the trust account is built and lost through the behaviors of all or even just a few of the people in the organization. Leaders play perhaps the most important role. Their decisions and actions affect people and teams on micro and macro levels.

The first level of trust is whether we ourselves are trustworthy people. Covey emphasizes that trustworthiness trust has two components: our *character* and our *competence*. These two terms are central to Covey's section on personal trustworthiness.

It is obvious that we cannot trust someone with a slimy character—dishonest, self-serving, egotistical, abusive, or cruel. Unfortunately, many leaders fall under that category. Even something as simple as micro-management tells others they are not trusted.

However, even if a person has the most sterling character, we still cannot trust them if they are incompetent at doing their jobs, whether managerial or technical. So, imagine the Venn diagram of two circles: character and competence. The intersection that belongs to both is the heart of our trustworthiness.

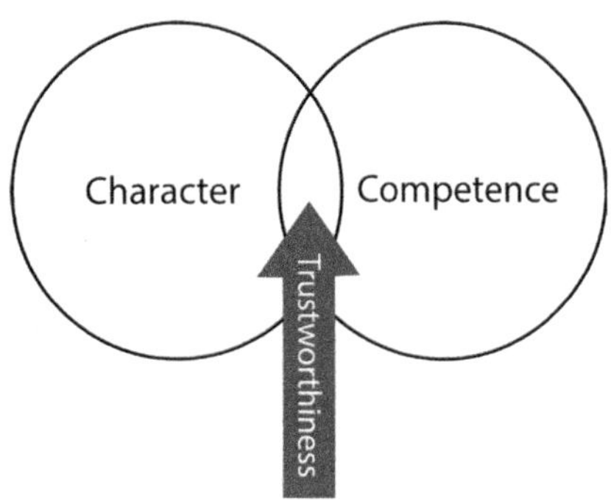

I have a friend who was an outstanding quarterback for a major university about 20 years ago. During that time, a new coach took over the team. When he arrived, the coach walked out onto the field privately with his quarterback and shared with him his goals and vision for the team. As they talked, the coach calmly threw footballs many yards down the field, into a garbage can. He did this over and over, not missing once. He showed his quarterback that he was competent. He could walk the talk. Imagine the trust impact this had on my friend.

At a memorial service for Stephen R. Covey, one of his daughters relayed a touching story about how she knew her father loved her and had a glimpse into his true character.

Because he often traveled out of town, Stephen would sometimes invite one of his nine children to accompany him. It was her turn to go with him to San Francisco, where he was giving a keynote address at major event. The thing she wanted to do most was go to a certain play, so her father bought them two tickets for the Wednesday evening performance. She was waiting quietly backstage for her father to finish his presentation.

He did not know that she could hear his discussion with a senior leader of a major corporation. The man wanted Stephen to meet and speak with his senior leaders from around the world on Wednesday night. This meeting could lead to an opportunity for them to use Stephen as a consultant. His daughter's heart sank when she heard this, but it skyrocketed upwards when she heard her father say, "I'm sorry, but I have another important commitment that night. Perhaps we can schedule it for some future day."

She said in her address that she sat on the floor and wept, knowing how important she was to her father and how important it was for him to keep his promise to her.

I once heard a powerful statement: *"What is important to another person should be as important to you as the other person is to you."*

Here are a few critical things to remember to build trust:

- Talk straight. Avoid double talk, passive aggressiveness, and other forms of pseudo-communication.
- Keep commitments.
- Be decisive and make smart decisions when they need to be made. You lose positive momentum by failing to make decisions when the moment is ripe. General George S. Patton said, "A less than perfect decision made in a timely manner is better than the best decision made too late." I find many weak leaders worm their

way out of making decisions that should be theirs by turning them over to committees or other people.

- Involve others in decisions that affect them.
- Show personal care and kindness. I heard that the Kansas City Chiefs coach, Andy Reid, knows the first names of everyone in his staff and team from janitors to quarterbacks. And they usually call him Andy!
- Hold yourself accountable first, others second.
- Deliver results. Action speaks louder than words and empty promises.
- Listen first, talk last. (Harrison Ford recently gave one of his secrets for a lasting marriage—"Don't talk, just nod.")
- Before taking any action or making any decision, ask yourself, *"What will this do to the level of trust?"*
- Keep learning, and don't be afraid to say that you don't know. Don't pretend to know something when you don't.
- Fix mistakes. You will make them. You can often build more trust after a mistake simply by how you admit it and correct it.
- Set the example. Be where the game is played. Show your staff you are not afraid to roll up your sleeves and do the arduous things.
- Set the example in work-life balance. Stay in shape physically, mentally, emotionally, and spiritually. Sharpen the saw.

Let us go forth and do all we can to build trust, first, by being trustworthy ourselves in both character and competence, and then by consciously working on all the behaviors that build trustworthiness. If we make a mistake and take withdrawals from the trust accounts of others, apologize and fix the mistake if we can. Show them that we have learned and will not repeat the mistake.

Of course, withdrawals can range from simple, easy-to-fix mistakes that only make a minor withdrawal to significant mistakes that make a serious withdrawal.

With simple mistakes, if we have consistently made trust deposits, the effect will be minor on the relationship. You can often earn greater trust than you had before the mistake if people see you genuinely fixing it and learning from it.

However, serious withdrawals, such as severe dishonesty, can completely drain the emotional bank account or trust account almost instantly. This isn't something that is easily recovered.

One example of trust being lost is when businesses start taking away benefits from trusting customers. This happened to me to a degree when an airline I had flown with for years starting to change its status rules. I had flown over a million miles with this airline and had top-tier status that came with some nice benefits. Then, this airline began to change the rules on how people earned the miles and status. They basically started to allow people to buy status through credit card purchases. Each year, this airline began to raise the annual fee to be a member of their "club." These changes certainly soured my trust and relationship with the airline.

Another personal example is from my wife, who enjoyed collecting baskets and liners from a prominent company in Ohio. This company has made hand-woven baskets for decades. They disappointed loyal customers when they began to outsource liners and décor to overseas providers. The company lost droves of buyers and distributors. Later, they recognized the mistake and brought the manufacturing closer to home, but, once trust and consumer confidence is lost, it may never be regained. Time will tell.

Another example is of a world-famous clam chowder outlet in California. People lined up for a block to buy the delicious chowder, which was quite pricey but worth every penny. One day, a new owner purchased the outlet and started watering down the chowder. Profits skyrocketed for a very brief time as production costs dropped. But the word got out, customers quit coming, and even though the restaurant brought back the original recipe, most customers had gone elsewhere. Trust was lost. I heard that the restaurant closed within two years.

These kinds of disasters can happen when decision-makers ignorantly or arrogantly think they can make what seem to be "minor" withdrawals from the trust accounts of clients, some of whom may be multi-generational. When it comes to trust withdrawals, people are rather unforgiving and may "vote with their feet" or "vote with their keystrokes," and companies lose millions of dollars or spend millions trying to regain the lost trust.

On the positive side, some of the biggest companies in the last twenty years, such as Amazon and Costco, have created high trust systems that consumers rely on. It amazes me that I can order something from Amazon and have it on my doorstep a day later. If I am unsatisfied, I can return the item for nearly any reason, unchallenged.

One personal Costco experience happened when I purchased a 500-megabyte storage device and gave it to my son. Many months later, the device failed him, and he called me when I was out of town. I advised him to take it back to the store. He himself was not a member of Costco, but that did not matter. He explained the problem and they gave him an even larger storage device at no cost. They told him to have a great day and to thank his father for being a loyal member. He walked out of Costco and called me, "Dad, Costco is AMAZING!" He now has a company of his own, has a Costco membership, and has spent many dollars there in the years since.

The moral of the story is before you make any business decision, or personal relationship action, *stop* and ask yourself, "What will this do to the trust we have?" If it will hurt the trust, *be aware* and stop yourself before it is too late or accept what the loss will incur. This sometimes happens when senior leaders and board members deliberately make decisions that they know will likely have long-term negative impact, but they know they can "take the money and run" before that happens or before stock values or profit margins fall.

In summary, trust is the hub of our helm, around which the other handles rotate. In high-trust cultures, people trust their leaders' vision and feel enrolled. High-trust systems and processes enable and engage individuals and teams. They will then feel motivated to explore new horizons. The ship sails smoothly.

So let us all consciously make decisions that add deposits to the trust accounts of our trusting family, friends, associates, and customers and reap the resulting benefits of trust.

In our next chapter, we will explore some of the things that can hinder the progress of our ship, using the analogy of barnacles!

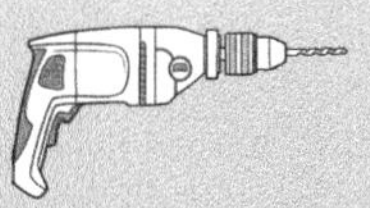

You might consider:

1. Contact FranklinCovey to set up the Trust Quotient (TQ) survey. This survey measures opinions and data on all the thirteen elements of trust. Follow up by taking your team through the Leading at the Speed of Trust workshop.

2. You can also contact us to run our no-cost Vital Signs Survey. It also has questions that delve into trust.

3. Bring your team or family members together and have an open and frank discussion on where and how trust could be improved. Do not get defensive. Just listen and learn.

4. When you make a mistake that erodes trust and creates a withdrawal from the emotional bank account or trust account of another, quickly apologize and seek ways to make amends. If you do this sincerely, it can add trust to the account and bring it higher than it ever was before. There is an old Chinese saying that says, "When you need to bow, bow deeply."

CHAPTER ELEVEN

Beware of the Barnacles!

In the days of wooden sailing ships, one of the great dangers was the buildup of barnacles on the ship's hull. Barnacles created a serious drag, which slowed the ship at sea. Barnacles also ate away at the wood and could eventually destroy a sailing ship. (The same thing can happen to modern boats when barnacles encrust the propellers.)

There were two main methods for removing barnacles. One was to raise the ship into a dry dock and laboriously scrape them off. This process was very labor intensive and hard on the wood.

The other method was to sail the ship into fresh water, like a river or inlet, and anchor it there. Because barnacles thrive best in saltwater, they would eventually die, dissolve, and drop off, leaving the hull clean and fresh.

There is an analogy here when it comes to organizations. Barnacles can gradually grow upon the symbolic hull of our company or organization. Some of these may be archaic policies, procedures, and systems. Others may be individuals who have become calcified and refuse to move, gradually creating drag on the progress of our organization. Remember our CAVEmen (Coworkers Against Virtually Everything)?

Ineffective or toxic people, processes, and systems eat away at the very foundation of our ship. Simply ignoring these deleterious barnacles is not the answer because they will eventually hinder or even destroy your organization.

In one of my favorite visual aids for my leadership presentations, I hold up an actual piece of fossilized dinosaur dung, called coprolite. It is likely over 70 million years old. I hold it up and humorously ask, "How much of this is hanging around in your organization." Archaic, nearly useless systems and processes!

There are two main types of these hindering barnacles: people and systems.

I previously mentioned the six-month fix or fire rule for the people barnacles. As a leader, if you have done all that you can do, following the Helm Model, and your crew members simply will not change or budge, follow the six-month rule. Do all you can to inspire and enable and engage them. Provide coaching and mentoring. Consider reassigning them to a crew-position more suitable to their temperaments and talents. But after six months, if it becomes clear that they have no intention to change and get on board, then it may be time to "free up their future," which is a kinder way to say, "fire them."

This kind of tough love is critical, not only for the organization but also for the individuals themselves because they are obviously not happy. They are not fitting in, and there could be a myriad of underlying reasons. These reasons might be personal problems in their lives or many other causes. They have basically quit and stayed. But freeing up their future might allow them a fresh start in a new career and the opportunity to find and follow an inner dream. That happened to me when I left my job to start my own company.

People are not the only barnacles. Other authors have said in various ways, "If you put really good people in really poor systems, the poor systems win every time."

When someone asks why you do something a certain way and the answer is, "We always have done it that way," you might have just found a possible barnacle!

Leaders must be consciously aware of these barnacles and inspect the ship for them. But it's not just leaders: everybody needs to be aware. This is where the exploring handle of our Helm Model comes into play.

It is tragic when the leadership itself becomes the most toxic barnacle. Other people see this and are frustrated by it, but they are helpless to do anything about it. So, returning to our two methods, we can pull the ship into the HR dry dock and use traditional HR processes to scrape off the toxic people, and leaders can go to work to scrape off policies and procedures. But the other method may be to symbolically sail the ship into freshwater and give a new vision that is clean and clear and fresh. Sometimes, organizations need to get out of the rough, crashing waves of the seas and pull in for a little while to rest and recover and get a new vision.

This may not take as long as you think, and it allows people to think of themselves and refresh themselves in the freshwater. Some toxic people barnacles may choose to drop off and go elsewhere. At all levels, others have a chance to pull away and look at the processes and systems that are holding up progress, loosen those barnacles, and let them drop off. One of the best ways to do this is to use focus groups.

Imagine what your organization could feel like when it is free of some of these barnacles and can sail more unencumbered into the future. This takes time and effort, but the return on investment can be significant.

In summary, all organizations and people have barnacles that limit, hinder, and impede their progress. I have identified only two main ones, people and systems, but I believe that by removing these barnacles progress is made a lot quicker.

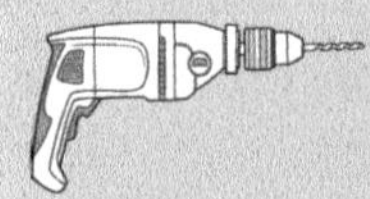

Application: Stop for a moment and examine your ship to see if barnacles are building up. As a leader, you may not see them or be aware of them, but they certainly are creating drag for your people. Conduct some focus groups or surveys to help identify them. Create task forces to address them and empower those task forces to take action to correct them. Think about a time or place of the symbolic freshwater that you can sail into. Take time to think and ponder to understand how to apply this principle.

CHAPTER TWELVE

Beware of the Dangerous Rocks!

"Look out ahead!" Those words have echoed down for centuries when lookouts, keeping an eye ahead, see rocks or icebergs or other hazards in the water. Perhaps they were sailors watching from high in a crow's nest atop a ship's mast or from others watching from the fo'c's'le of a ship. Some of the greatest dangers their ships faced were rocks or icebergs. Some were readily visible, peeking above the surface of the water, but others were hidden under the waves. These hidden hazards were perhaps even more dangerous with the potential to rip into the hulls of the ships.

Such was the terrible fate of the RMS Titanic in the early morning hours of April 15, 1912, only four days into her maiden voyage from Southampton, England, to New York City. Of the 2,224 people on board, more than 1,500 died when the ship sank, making it one of the deadliest peacetime maritime disasters in history.

Much has been written about the disaster, with much of the blame attached to her captain, Edward John Smith. Smith was determined to set a record for crossing the Atlantic and ignored six warnings of sea ice. Traveling at 41 km/hr, the Titanic hit an iceberg. The glancing blow tore open enough of the watertight compartments to flood the ship.

As individuals and organizations, we must also be very wary of the symbolic rocks and icebergs that can damage or sink our lives or organizations. I will cover just a few.

1. **Ego and Self-interest:** Few things get in the way more than leaders or anyone having their ego or desire for self-interest as the dominant drive. *Do not let being right get in the way of doing right.* This seemed to be one factor in Captain Smith's character: his determination to ignore warnings and go full speed ahead was a deadly flaw.

2. **Fixed versus Abundant Mindset:** Having a fixed mindset means you see things in only a certain way and are resistant to new ideas. It is like a pie that is fixed in shape to the pan. Giving a larger slice to someone means a smaller slice for you or others. Those with an abundant mindset are open to new ideas. They see the pie as having a stretchable border, and sharing means the pie gets larger for everyone.

The Titanic had boastfully been labeled unsinkable, and this was part of the officer's fixed mindset.

3. **Lack of Vision:** This was addressed earlier in the envision chapter. Vision is critical, but it also needs to be fluid and able to change.

4. **Competition Making You Irrelevant:** This point is illustrated by the companies that manufactured buggy whips in the early 1900's. When the automobile was introduced, everything changed. Buggy whips became obsolete. A more recent example is the story of BlackBerry, mentioned in a previous chapter on problem solving. It was the first true multi-functional cell phone that could also text, read emails, and interface with the newly emerging internet. It was introduced in 1999 and took the market by storm. At one time, it was the dominating must-have device and a status symbol. By September 2011, there were 85 million BlackBerry users worldwide. However, with the introduction of Android and iOS platforms, dominated by the new iPhone, there was a three-quarter decline in users. Blackberry tried to play catch-up by releasing Android-based versions, but it was too late. On 18 February 2022, the company shut down.

5. **Self-deception:** Individuals and companies can easily become self-addicted to previous success and deceive themselves into failing to see the writing on the wall. Such was the example of the Swiss watchmakers from a previous chapter. We can see this self-deception played out in the story of the Titanic. From the manufacturers to the inspectors and the captain and the crew, self-deception and believing she was unsinkable led to disaster.

6. **Failure to See Looming Change and Shortsightedness:** Like self-deception, this short-sighted mindset can deny and refuse to see the upcoming changes in the market and consumer demands. It is being too short-sighted to see or accept other dangers that could be lurking ahead. This can lead to a certain cockiness, as when Columbus had turned over the helm of the Santa Maria to a young man of little experience. The ship ran aground in Hispaniola.

7. **Running Out of Fuel:** *Fuel* here simply means the resources needed to continue to be successful. The danger here is when companies expand too quickly and are unable to maintain the momentum that brought their initial success. This almost happened with Starbucks when it opened too many stores too quickly, and quality and sales declined. Luckily, the leaders saw the error, regrouped, reorganized, and shut down many stores.

8. **Lack of PMCS (Preventative Maintenance Checks and Services):** This is a military term that emphasizes the need for constant monitoring of maintenance, particularly in equipment. It introduces constant preventative maintenance through frequent checks and excellent services.

Interestingly, research on the steel used in the hull of the Titanic shows that in the rush to build the ship, the metal was not tested to the temperatures of the North Sea. The metal was too brittle to stand the blow of the iceberg.

In summary, as we sail our ships, we must be constantly alert to the possible dangers in the waters ahead. Ego, self-deception, fixed mindsets, and short-sightedness can bring disaster as it did that freezing April morning in 1912.

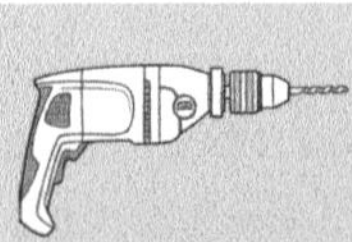

Watch out for these icebergs and rocks and continue full steam ahead.

1. Consider contacting us to run a survey that will help you identify areas that are possible icebergs.

2. Pull a focus group together to discuss these and other possible dangers and see what your staff, customers, and others consider the danger points on your ship's hull. Use them to figure out how you can strengthen the armor plating.

3. Are you so immersed in the past and your past ways of doing things that you are perhaps blissfully unaware of danger points or ignoring changes in the marketplace? There may be opportunities if you sail into some fresh water.

CHAPTER THIRTEEN

Customers Only Want Two Things

In this chapter, I will briefly summarize the concept covered in depth in my book, *Customers Only Want Two Things: Winning Loyalty in a Competitive World.*

Like the *Leaders Do Five Things* concept, winning customer loyalty can also be simplified. Customers ultimately want two things: 1) Solve My Problem, and 2) Leave Me Feeling Great about the Experience.

Solving the customer's problem is a basic need. All businesses, products, and services exist because there is a problem to solve. If humans or organizations had no problems, there would be no need for businesses, products, or services. Solving the problem is what customers or clients *expect.* Simply solving the problem will likely lead to customer *satisfaction* but not customer *loyalty.* And the difference is huge and is crucial to your success. But the reality is that similar businesses or products can likely do the same thing. How many restaurants can you visit in your city for a satisfactory meal?

This epiphany is explained in a great book by Jeffrey Gittomer, *Customer Satisfaction is Worthless: Customer Loyalty is Priceless.* I expanded on this concept in my book.

Loyal customers do four things: 1) they come back, 2) they use more of your services or buy more, 3) they refer others, and 4) they care enough to offer critical feedback. If these things happen often in your business, it is a sign that you are winning loyalty.

A second book, *The Ultimate Question* by Fred Reichheld, is equally mind-opening. He introduced a simple question that helps you determine if your customers are detractors, passives, or promoters: *"On a scale of zero to ten, how likely is it you would recommend our business to a friend or family member?"* (It can be worded differently depending on several factors.)

Those who give you a zero to six are *detractors*. Depending on how unhappy they are, they can even become adversaries to your success. Who would go to a restaurant if your friend gave the food and service a rating of zero to six?

Those who give you a seven or eight are *passive*. They may or may not recommend you but are not necessarily for or against you. This equates to getting a C or B on a report card!

What we want are customers who give you a nine or ten. These are *promoters* and are almost certain to do some or all four of the four things loyal customers do. By subtracting the percentage of detractors from the percentage of promoters you get your Net Promoter Score (NPS). It ranges from -100 to 100. The best performers out there have NPS scores well above 70.

The power of this measurement lies in simplicity. I cannot count the number of times I get surveys from companies that ask too many questions. I once stayed in a hotel of a major hotel chain, and the survey I got a week later was several pages long on my computer. Now, I usually delete such surveys. They ask too much, too late. The only people who take the time to answer these are probably very unhappy. So, most people delete them.

Using this simple zero to ten question gives you the basis for computing loyalty. It is best done on the spot while the memory is fresh in the minds of your customers, not a week later like my hotel experience. You can follow it up with a simple, optional question, *"Why did you give us that score?"*

The customer can then tell you what is most important for you to hear: what is most important in their minds at the time of service. Note: if you added two other open-ended questions, they could be, *"What did we do well?"* and *"What can we do differently?"*

To summarize, your one and only goal is to win as many promoters as possible. You can never satisfy some people, but there are things you can do that win loyalty and get you the nine or ten rating promoters give you.

Remember: You cannot focus on or stop at mere satisfaction. Do your best to solve the customer's true problem. You must go beyond this and leave them feeling great about the experience. Not just good, but *great.*

If you want to learn how to do this, I hope you will read my book or consider taking your team through my workshop. I have packed these with dozens of ideas and examples, many of which are rather easy to implement and leave an indelible impression in the minds of your customers. Loyalty is a very strong emotion, and for good or bad it can be easily lost.

All I want to do in this chapter is plant a basic understanding of this concept, and, to relate a corollary question that can be asked of your employees, *"How likely is it you would recommend working for us to a friend or family member?"*

The staff that respond with a nine or ten are much more likely to be motivated, stay with you, and recommend you to others. Winning loyalty reduces turnover and improves morale, motivation, and inwardly driven performance. The resulting equation is the Employee Net Promoter Score (eNPS). There is a proven correlation between the eNPS and the NPS.

I place this concept in your mind as you read this book. Nothing I know of positively influences the eNPS more than great leadership! Leaders win the loyalty of their staff by also solving problems *and* going beyond, leaving them feeling great about working for you. This happens as you progress through the Helm Model: envision, enroll, enable, engage, explore, and base the revolution on the power of the axis of trust.

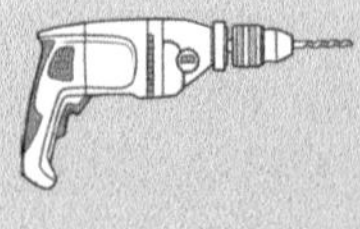

Application Ideas

1. Go forth and focus your time, energy, resources, and training on ways to win loyalty, and your success is almost assured.

2. Consider conducting a NPS survey of your customers and an ENPS survey of all your staff. Then, go to work to improve these scores.

3. Contact us if you want us to set up a customer loyalty survey for you.

CHAPTER FOURTEEN

The Multiplying Force of Love

"I have decided to stick to love.... Hate is too heavy a burden to bear." —Martin Luther King, Jr.

"Darkness cannot drive out darkness; only light can do that. Hate cannot drive out hate; only love can do that." —Martin Luther King Jr.

With his wise words, Dr. King is inviting us all to let go of hate—hate for others, for things, and even for ourselves. Replace hate with love as much as possible, for love is, perhaps, the greatest force multiplier of all.

It is fitting to end with the concept of love as the final chapter of this book on leadership. Just like leadership, more has been written about love than perhaps any other thing. It is written in songs and poems to essays, research papers, and entire books. Throughout the ages, the power of love has resonated far deeper than hate.

This inestimable power of love brings tremendous outcomes, even in places like sports. I previously mentioned how a sports commentator wrote about the Kansas City Chiefs football coach Andy

Reid: "He loves his players, and they love him." Several players who were interviewed said they would do anything for Coach Reid.

"Love recognizes no barriers. It jumps hurdles, leaps fences, penetrates walls to arrive at its destination full of hope." —Maya Angelou

---

I am unabashedly Christian and uphold Jesus Christ as the greatest, most brilliant, visionary, and self-sacrificing leader of all time. His great love led him to suffer in Gethsemane and die on Calvary. He taught about the power of love. In John 13:34–35, he said: A new commandment I give unto you, That ye love one another; as I have loved you, that ye also love one another. By this shall *all* men know that ye are my disciples, if ye have love one to another.

I have long been inspired by the remarkable life story of Corrie Ten Boom. Boom was incarcerated in one of the terrible Nazi death camps with some of her family, some of whom did not survive. Her story illustrates how the power of love sustained her through the terrible experience, and she went on to lecture and write for years. She profoundly illustrates how her choice to love, not hate, kept her and others alive.

After concluding a lecture after the war, she was approached by one of the guards who had abused her and others in the death camp. He told her how glad he would be if she could forgive him.

She recalls that she stopped momentarily and thought, "How can I forgive this man?" She silently prayed and asked God to lend her His love for that man. Her heart was filled with that love, and she frankly forgave him. Hate was simply a burden too heavy to bear.

Recently, my wife and I read two books on love. One written by the great football quarterback, Steve Young, entitled *The Law of Love*. In it, he outlines several principles for unleashing the power of love. One of his concepts we learned is to not have transactional love, meaning you love with an expectation that the other person will love back as if love is a transaction. Instead, love unconditionally, with no outward or inward expectation that something will come back to you.

One story he tells is how one of the opposing players, a friend of his, would violently sack him, hold out his hand, pat him on the back, and ask, "Hey Steve, how is your family?" His point is that we often must do hard things, but there are ways to integrate love into most of them.

The second book, by Dr. John and Julie Gottman, is titled *The Love Prescription*. Backed by thousands of hours of research, their claim is that applying principles of patient, understanding love can heal many, if not most, marriages and other relationships. Their book is power-packed with research and dozens of practical examples. They have a seven-day prescription of things to do to restore love in a relationship:

1. Make contact.
2. Ask a big question.
3. Say thank you.
4. Give a real compliment.
5. Ask for what you need.
6. Reach out and touch.
7. Declare a date night.

They filled this relatively short 150-page book with dozens of practical ways to do all seven things. While most are applied to marriage and family, many cross into any leadership or relationship. For instance, a "date night" could mean taking a work partner out to lunch to make contact, ask good questions, thank them, and the other prescriptions.

In my work with leaders and teams, I often observe leaders who feel that to make someone or a team do better, they need to make sure they feel worse. I am sure you have experienced or seen this yourself. The higher way is love. When people feel genuinely loved, they are free from the need to defend themselves and instead turn their desire, minds, and creativity to working out solutions on their own or with your kind guidance—something to think about.

One final thought: perhaps a key foundation to this ability to love others comes first from self-love. Jesus Christ famously taught in Matthew 22:35–39:

> Then one of them, which was a lawyer, asked him a question, tempting him, and saying, Master, which is the

> great commandment in the law? Jesus said unto him, Thou shalt love the Lord thy God with all thy heart, and with all thy soul, and with all thy mind. This is the first and great commandment. And the second is like unto it, Thou shalt love thy neighbor as thyself.

Note his enjoinder: "as thyself." If you are like me, you have likely found it easier to love others than to love yourself. We usually are our greatest critic of ourselves.

The dilemma of military leadership was said by General Robert E. Lee, "To be a great general, you have to love the army and then order the death of the thing you love." (Luckily, such a terrible dichotomy does not apply to most situations.)

Even at the end, when his army surrendered to the Union and General Lee rode past his soldiers, they took off their hats and said, "If you give us the word, we will keep fighting." In another instance, he was finally asleep in his tent at night when hundreds of his soldiers had to march past. When they were told he was asleep, they removed their boots, kept their rifles and equipment from clanking, and quietly passed by.

"The size of a leader is determined by the depth of his convictions, the height of his ambitions, the breadth of his vision, and the reach of his love." —D. N. Jackson

---

One sweet example of the power of healing love happened to me as a 17-year-old. I had been hopelessly in love with my first girlfriend. I even imagined myself eventually marrying her!

One morning before school, she sent her best friend over to my house to give me a message: "It's over." My world fell apart in a moment. I never had felt heartache or pain like that. I remember driving my Jeep out into the hills above Redlands, California, determined never to go back to school again. I wondered if I had enough gas to get to Mexico. I wept and wept until there were no tears left. I drove slowly home, skipped dinner, and went straight to bed.

The door slowly opened, and my father, Frank Miller, quietly entered. He pulled back the covers of my bed and climbed in beside me. He wrapped his strong arms around me and held me closer than perhaps I had ever been held before. Of course, that brought more tears of release. He held me, saying nothing until my sobs started to subside. Then, he simply said, "My son, I love you. I promise the sun will come out again."

Then he left. And the sun did come out and I went to school in time to see my ex-girlfriend walking hand in hand with my now-former best friend. I lost both in one day.

My father was an ex-Army colonel, a veteran of World War II, and could have told me to shape up, snap out of it, be a man, etc. But instead, he held me. Such is the power of love.

"Love is a verb. Love—the feeling—is the fruit of love, the verb or our loving actions. —Stephen R. Covey

---

Final thoughts

"Let what you love drive what you do" (*Argyle*, 2023).

"Though we are incomplete, God loves us completely. Though we are imperfect, He loves us perfectly. Though we may feel lost and without a compass, God's love encompasses us completely.... He loves every one of us, even those who feel flawed, rejected, awkward, sorrowful, or broken." —Dieter F. Uchtdorf

"There is comfort in the strength of love; 'Twill make a thing endurable, which else would overset the brain, or break the heart." —William Wordsworth

As I conclude this chapter, I invite you to think back on the most powerful and motivating leader you experienced and see if this chapter is self-proving. They probably inspired you to levels of greatness you never dreamed of, but they did it, in part, with the force multiplier of love.

Then go forth and ask yourself in any given situation, "How can I demonstrate a deep, caring love for this person or in this moment?" Even when we are called upon to correct or adjust, there is almost always a way to do it in a way that communicates love.

Now on to the Toolbox

In the sections ahead, I will outline ten tools you can put into your Leadership Toolbox. These tools somewhat align with the six parts of the Helm Model, but most of them apply to more than one handle. Here is a general alignment. I hope you can cherry-pick those tools that are most valuable to you. Sail on!

Tool	Helm Model
Tool One: Developing Strategic Plans	Envision and Explore
Tool Two: Hiring for Success	Enroll, Enable, and Engage
Tool Three: Onboarding—Energy and Focus from the Start	Enroll, Engage, and Trust
Tool Four: Leading Great Meetings	Engage, Explore, and Trust
Tool Five: Working with Difficult Crew Members	Enable, Engage, and Trust
Tool Six: Leading and Working with the Generations	Enable, Engage, and Trust
Tool Seven: Understanding and Leading Men and Women	Enable, Engage, and Trust
Tool Eight: Building and Leading a Service Culture	Enable, Engage, and Trust
Tool Nine: Suggested Reading List	All
Tool Ten: Great Quotes	All
Tool Eleven: How VisionBound Can Help	All

TOOL NUMBER ONE

Developing Strategic Plans

Chapter Five outlined how to create your mission, vision, values, and measures of success. With these creations firmly in place, you now have the all-important *why* in place. It is time to use these to drive the *how* of a solid strategic plan.

Strategic thinking and planning can and should be a complex and detailed process. You are trying to envision the future as far as three to five years in advance and create strategic lanes, goals, and milestones to reach this future. It has been said that the best way to predict your future is to create it. That is the process of strategic planning. (I offer my service to guide your team through this process if you desire.)

Rudy Giuliani popularized an old axiom often used in the military: *Hope is not a strategy.* I am a strong believer in the power of hope: it gets us up and going in the morning, and when people or organizations individually or collectively lose hope, they are on a fast or slow glide to failure. That said, hope is never a good strategy. Simply hoping your sales will increase, your people will become more engaged, or your business or relationships survive is not the answer. With your inspiring purpose fixed in your senses, it is time to create a plan to execute!

We return to that great quote by Barack Obama: "The best way to not feel hopeless is to get up and do something. Don't wait for good things to happen to you. If you go out and make some good things happen, you will fill the world with hope, you will fill yourself with hope."

But neither can we go out randomly firing away without clearly aligning our goals and actions with a relevant and doable strategy. As the old Arab proverb says, "The eagle that chases two rabbits catches neither."

Effective strategic planning aims to determine what rabbits to chase and clearly focus on the most important ones.

One useful way is to utilize the 4P's: people, product, process, and performance.

- **People:** In your strategic plan and operations, selecting and onboarding the right people is essential. Ultimately, your people are those who will carry out the plan. The next two tools will address interviewing and onboarding top talent.
- **Product:** No amount of great people, great systems, great marketing, or a great sales team will succeed if your products or services are outdated, ineffective, or do not meet the customer's needs.
- **Process:** Great strategic plans also address the processes needed to drive success, from your production to your delivery.
- **Performance:** Hopefully, if your people, products, and processes are aligned and effective, the result will be great performance.

One way to illustrate this strategic planning process is to envision a three-lane highway with three lanes moving forward: strategic, operational, and tactical. To illustrate this further, I will use a simple military analogy that can apply to almost any business or endeavor:

- **Strategic:** Fight the right battle.
- **Operational:** Fight the right battle at the right place at the right time with the right people and the right stuff.
- **Tactical:** Fight the battle right!

I was involved somewhat in the military operation of Desert Storm as an active-duty Major in the United States Army. Let me illustrate these three lanes with this scenario.

Strategic Lane: The vision or goal was to hopefully defeat the threat of Saddam Hussein and other forces post 9/11. High-level political and military leaders determined that the strategy (fight the right battle) was to engage enemy forces in Iraq and Afghanistan with a combination of military force and economic and political pressure. (History will validate or invalidate that strategy that has resulted in the longest war in American history.)

Operational Lane: Once the right battle had been identified, thousands of operations kicked in to "fight the right battle at the right time, right place, with the right people and the right stuff." This involved logistics, personnel, training, equipment, transportation, and the myriad of operational details to launch a full-scale combat operation, along with the economic and political lines. From a personal standpoint, this is where my work kicked in as a logistician.

Tactical Lane: All of this planning would have been a failure and virtually moot if our warfighters could not "fight the battle right." If they could not use their weapons and training properly nor handle the stress and intensity of ground, air, and sea combat, all the strategy and operational planning would be useless.

Sooner or later, it is the boots on the ground that win wars. And sooner or later, despite all your strategic planning and goals it is your boots on the ground that carry it out.

While this is a military example, it has applications to most other human endeavors in businesses, non-profits, and even families. According to data from the Bureau of Labor Statistics (BLS), approximately 20% of new businesses fail during the first two years of being open, 45% during the first five years, and 65% during the first ten years. Only 25% of new businesses make it to fifteen years or more. These statistics haven't changed much over time and have been consistent since the 1990s.

According to the BLS study, entrepreneurs started 774,725 new businesses in the year ending March 2019. From the historical data, we can expect approximately 155,000 of those businesses to fail within the first two years. According to research by Michael Deane, cited in Investopedia, the main reasons new businesses fail are 1) they are not investigating the market, 2) they have business plan problems, 3) they have too little financing, 4) they have a bad location, internet presence, and marketing, 5) they are remaining rigid, and 6) they are expanding too fast.

These failure points have their basis primarily in a failure to think and plan strategically. Having an exciting new product or idea and blithely expecting it to succeed is the "hope is not a strategy" approach.

The terrible months of the COVID-19 pandemic have seen the downfall of many companies, large and small. Those who survived and even thrived may well be those who can adjust their vision and mission and create a flexible, innovative new strategy.

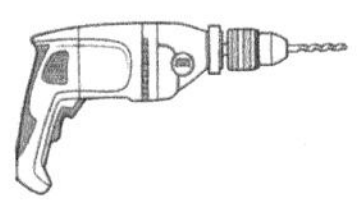

My purpose here is not to delve further into the mechanics of strategic planning: that would be a book by itself and there are many good ones you can read. But I can provide you with lists of questions I have developed to help you think deeply enough in the three lanes:

Strategic Planning: "Fight the right battle."

Concept Questions

1. Are we in the right markets?
2. Do we have the right products for today's market?
3. Are we developing products/services for tomorrow's market?
4. What is the equivalent of Sony's Walkman in our market, and how do we discover and develop it?
5. Are we positioned to be successful ten years from now?
6. Is our vision statement clear, compelling, and relevant?
7. Are we actively pursuing succession planning?
8. Can our people think strategically?
9. Are we expanding too quickly? Too slowly?
10. Are we aligned with our core values? Are we abandoning any?
11. Do we "know the enemy," and are we maneuvering accordingly?
12. What will customers want in one year, five years, ten years?
13. What won't they want?
14. Are we training for the future, not just now?
15. What new products and services do we need?
16. How are customers changing?

17. How does our reward and compensation program need to change to motivate the creation of a new future?

18. How will we get the information we need?

19. How must we change our structure and organization to be strategically set for the future?

20. Do our people at all levels understand the big picture of our strategy and vision to operate independently, guided by the vision?

Operational Planning: "Fight the right battle at the right time, in the right place, with the right folks and the right stuff."

Concept Questions

1. Do we have the right organizational structure in place to be both effective and efficient?
2. Do we have the right folks on the bus?
3. Do we have the right folks in the right seats on the bus?
4. Is our mission statement clear, compelling, inspiring, and concise? Does it guide what we do each day and help us make operational decisions?
5. Do we reward the right folks for doing the right stuff? Are we rewarding what we want? Problem-solving rather than problem-finding? Creative thinking and risk taking?
6. Are we doing the right thing in the right way at the right time for the right reasons?
7. Are we positioned in the right place in the market, geographically, demographically, and culturally?
8. Do we have the right financial resources, and are they targeted at the right products and markets? Pareto's Rule?
9. Are we concentrating on the "low-hanging fruit"?
10. Do we have the right equipment for the current battle, and how long will it stay current?
11. Are we structured properly and organized properly so our team can work effectively?
12. Do our work processes make sense, or do they frustrate our people?
13. Does the right information get to the right folks at the right time?
14. Are we empowering our people? Do they feel ownership?

15. Are our meetings both efficient and effective? Do we have too many? Are the right people involved?

16. Are our products and services getting out just on time, or are our processes too cumbersome?

17. Are the right rewards in place to provide the right incentives?

Tactical Planning: "Fight the Battle Right"

Concept Questions

1. Are our people properly technically trained?

2. Are they trained in communication, relationship building, and customer service?

3. Do we have strong emerging leaders?

4. Do they know how to use our equipment efficiently and safely?

5. Are we training them for the future? Cross training?

6. Do we know how to make our products properly, balancing quality with safety and cost-efficiency?

7. Does our equipment operate well? Is our maintenance up to standards?

8. Do our folks know how to react to problems flexibly? Can they operate independently, or are they overly dependent on management?

9. Have we set good action plans? Do people have a clear idea of what to do and why each day?

10. Are we empowering our people? Do they feel ownership?

11. Is our ordering and shipping system cost-efficient and effective from a customer's point of view?

12. Do our processes make sense to our customers? How frustrated would we be if we were one of our customers?

13. Is our turnover too high to allow us to be effective and efficient? If so, why are our people leaving? Would you want to work for the company in an entry position?

14. Are our people allowed to do their jobs with a minimum (but just the right amount) of supervision and control?

15. Do our people feel abandoned to face problems alone?

When you have thought through and carefully researched the answers to many of these questions, you are more prepared for the process of strategic planning.

My approach with my clients is to help them create a wall map of the three lanes and the actions for who does what, by when, and how they should follow up in columns in each of the three lanes. The result is a clear picture of how the strategy drives the operational and tactical elements in each lane. The rows represent various aspects of the operation. There is an example of a map at the end of this chapter. You can contact us to order a wall map.

Now comes one critical step: Boil down all of this, including a general strategic plan, into a two-page document, easy to understand at the 8th-grade level. Avoid jargon and acronyms that many staff would not understand. I recommend a bullet format that outlines the strategy in six-month increments (but do not give away trade secrets that competitors might find advantageous.)

Start at the top with the vision, mission, values, and measures of success. Then, outline the strategic plan to achieve these in general terms, and end with major WIGs (Wildly Important Goals) that will achieve the strategy and mission. Brief this to each team and discuss it with everyone to help them create their own individual contribution plan (ICP).

The result should be that anyone from the top of the organization to the bottom can stand in front of the wall chart and see how their part relates to the rest.

In summary, it has wisely been said that poor planning prevents poor performance. Yet, great planning starts with a well-developed strategic plan that is then executed through the operational and tactical lanes outlined in this tool.

The next two tools address hiring and onboarding.

Instructions for the Strategic/Operational/Tactical Wall Chart: The final chart should be at least six feet wide but that size may vary to make it all fit. The Project and Remarks columns should be about six inches wide. There should be four inches between line (large enough for the square Post-it notes to fit). Use three different colored notes for the three lanes. You may order a chart by contacting us at info@visionbound.com.

	Strategic "Fight the right battle"				**Operational** "Fight the right battle at the right time, in the right place, with the right folks and the right stuff."				**Tactical** "Fight the battle right."				Remarks
Project	**Who**	**Does What**	**By When**	**How Follow-up**	**Who**	**Does What**	**By When**	**How Follow-up**	**Who**	**Does What**	**By When**	**How Follow-up**	
Practice Row for Exercise: Think of a project or program you are about to undertake and fill in the rows below. Who, does what, by when, strategically, operationally, or tactically?													

TOOL NUMBER TWO

Hiring for Success

Behavior Based Job Interviews

"You're only as good as the people you hire."
—Ray Kroc, founder of McDonald's

In the chapter on enrolling, I addressed the importance of getting the right people on board, and that process usually begins with effective hiring and job interviews. So, let's learn how to do more effective interviews.

Remember that while you are interviewing a person, they are also interviewing you and the team to get a sense of whether your organization is a place they would like to join.

Whether or not you end up hiring them, you want them to leave with a clear understanding of the organization's vision, mission, and purpose and a good feeling in their hearts and minds about who you are and what you do. If you hire them, the interview can be a great and exciting kick-off.

Anyone who watched the movie *Forrest Gump* might remember the iconic scene where Forest is sitting on a park bench with a box of chocolates on his knee. He wisely tells a person sitting next to him, "Life is like a box of chocolates—you never know what you're going to get."

That is true in interviews if you hire mostly from a person's resume. I once heard the statement, "There are lies, damn lies, and *resumes*." If you don't interview deeply and thoroughly to get an understanding of the whole person, you may be surprised who shows up for work on the first day, month, or year. Experience shows prevention is better than a cure. It is much easier to get the right people on board than it is to have to free up their future or deal with their antics or poor performance later.

I once went to lunch with the HR director of Southwest Airlines. She told me how their company has become known for the unique, bright, and fun nature of their personnel and their work culture. She told me, "We hire for attitude and train for skill."

A fun nature and great interpersonal skills are important for even their pilots. I once flew a Southwest flight, and the plane started to bounce around in very strong turbulence. I could sense the stress in the passengers around us. Suddenly, the voice of the pilot and the copilot came from the front of the plane, together singing a variation on the theme song from *Gilligan's Island:* "The weather started getting rough, the tiny plane was tossed. If not for the courage of the fearless crew (inserting their names), your lunch might be lost!"

People were cracking up all around me. As I said in the beginning, culture is created predominately by people.

My purpose now is not to provide an extensive treatise on how to do job interviews but to provide a few tips to help you get the right people on board.

First, and this is very important, you do not want to waste your time or their time. So, once they sit down, give a brief description of the position for which you are interviewing them, including enough detail. Then, ask them, "Are you interested in this position as described?"

There is a possibility that the person was misinformed and that the position was much different in their minds. That gives them an escape pod and saves you time as well.

You might then continue by describing the company and share with them its mission statement and purpose. This puts people at ease, and you can begin getting a sense of their personality and energy. Ask them why they would like to be a part of this mission, how they see themselves in this purpose, and what talents they could bring to the team. This creates a positive start to the rest of the interview.

The key to the whole process is something we can refer to as behavioral-based interviewing. I will illustrate with a couple of simple examples. Let's imagine you are in an interview, and you ask the lame question, "Do you think you get along well with people?" Or even worse, "Do you like people?" *Who is going to say they don't?* (Even Hannibal Lecter, the clinically insane cannibal in *Silence of the Lambs*, likes people—cooked in various ways!)

Change it to a behavior-based question such as, "Tell me about your favorite coworker you have ever worked with and what you liked about them?" Then, ask a contrary evidence question, "Now tell me about a time when you did *not* get along with someone at work and how you resolved it." You can even dig a little deeper and ask them to provide some specific examples of what happened.

A second example would be asking, "Will you come in to work on time?" Instead, turn into a behavior-based question that requires a demonstration— "Can you show me how you organize your time?"

If they have a paper planner or an electronic device, ask them to walk you through how they organized their time this week. You could also ask, "Tell me about a recent busy week when you had a lot of conflicts and demands for your time and energy. How did you prioritize and work it all out?"

In these kinds of questions, you are asking people to describe their actual *behaviors* in certain situations with real-world examples requiring thought. They cannot give a simple yes or no.

Note: Before heading into these questions, you might tell them, "I'm going to be asking you some questions that will require some thought. Please take some time and answer when you're ready." Once you've asked a question, don't stare at them—busy yourself until they are ready.

Other examples of good behavior-based questions might be:

"Tell me about a time when you did not agree with your boss on an important issue. How did you resolve it?"

"What was the most challenging thing you have ever done in your career or your life?"

"At what times in your life do you feel the most fulfillment and joy?" Or ask the opposite: "At what times in your life do you feel the most stress and least fulfillment?"

When selecting these questions, match them to the type of position the person will be in. For instance, if the person will be interacting directly with your customers in a sales position or as a receptionist, you might ask: "Tell me about a time when you had to work with a particularly difficult customer. What was the situation, and how did you deal with it? What was the final outcome?"

If the person is going to be working on a technical project team, you might ask a different question: "Describe a recent technical project which you led or participated in successfully. What was the outcome, and what was your role in it?"

A balancing contrary evidence question might follow: "Please tell me about a time when you feel you or your team was not successful in a project and what did you learn from it?"

If you want a complete list of many behavior-based questions, please go to the tool section of our website or contact us at info@visionbound.com.

Here are some other ideas on how to conduct a great interview:

1. Set the stage. Kindly invite the person in and offer them a bottle of water. Try not to sit directly behind a desk. If you need writing space, sit at the corner of your desk so that most of your body is turned toward the person being interviewed. It's important to be able to take notes but keep in mind that it makes people a little nervous to see you writing a lot. Try to keep most of your thoughts in your mind and jot them down later. You can even ask the person if it's okay to record the interview so that you can refer to it later. Having these recordings is also a protection in case the person comes back later and claims that you were somehow biased by their answers. It happens!

Note: This brings up an issue that sometimes happens when people volunteer information you did not specifically ask for. For instance, a woman might mention that she is pregnant, even though you did not ask her whether she was or anything about her family situation.

I read a case where a woman was not hired after being interviewed. She came back with a lawyer and claimed that she was not chosen because she was pregnant. She won because there was no proof otherwise. This is where the recording of the interview would be ideal, but if you do not have a recording, simply stop and say, "I am happy for you, but please note that I did not ask for that information, and you volunteered it. I'm making a note of that. It will not have any bearing on whether we hire you or not." A panel of interviewers provides two or more witnesses as well.

You might want to do an interview search for illegal or improper interview questions.

2. Once you have your questions, I suggest you write them on the following form in the first column below. You can download the full form in the tools section of our website: www.VisionBound.com

Selection Interview Worksheet

Candidate: ________ **Interviewer:** ________ **Date:** ______

Revelant Job Skill or Requirement	Notes and Evaluation
Example: **Quality/Skill: Decisiveness**	*He made a tough budget decision . . . used outside experts. Impressed.*
Question: *Describe a tough decision you had to make when there was no governing policy*	**Response** 1 2 3 4 5 **Delivery** 1 2 3 4 5
Quality/Skill: **Question:**	
	Response 1 2 3 4 5 **Delivery** 1 2 3 4 5

3. In the column on the right, you evaluate the person on a scale of 1 to 5 on two things: the quality of their response and the quality of how well they delivered it.

For instance, the content of their answer might not be ideal, but maybe they delivered it with confidence and clarity. This shows that they can think on their feet and are poised. Those qualities may be essential in a customer-facing job position.

Note that it may be nice to let people know ahead of time to be prepared for these questions by thinking about instances in their life where they have been successful or unsuccessful at work. Alternatively, you might decide to give them no warning just to see how well they handle it.

If you have specific expectations, you might tell the interviewee about them when you invite them to the interview: "Please be here promptly at 3 o'clock in business dress."

The last tip I want to give you is to use a panel interview in some situations. Perhaps have two or three other people there to help answer questions and rate the answers. It is a little more intimidating for the interviewee to face more people, so put them at ease by telling them this is a very important position and you want a balanced viewpoint. Including a woman or minority on the panel adds critical diversity. So does inviting someone who would be working with them as a team member.

During the interview, rotate asking the questions among panel members, but everyone does the scoring on every question on the sheet I showed above. Afterward, the panel can get together and discuss their opinions and ratings. This can also help provide second and third witnesses to what happened in the interview in case of a legal challenge.

Finally, thank the person for their time and tell them exactly when and how they will be informed of the decision: "We will let you know between three and 4 o'clock on Friday by telephone."

It is a courtesy that the person be informed by the interviewer. If the news is good and you are hiring the person, it is nice to tell them why you were impressed with them and how glad you will be to have them on board. If not, be careful not to go into details about why the person was not selected. Simply say, "The decision was difficult, and we had many qualified applicants like you, so we made a decision on another who would be the best fit for us at this time." If you were impressed with the person, you could ask, "Would you like to be considered for other positions in the future?"

The purpose of this process is twofold. First, you want to get the right people on board. But you also want to leave them impressed with your professionalism and the kindness and care you showed them in the interview. You want them to leave with a very positive impression of the company itself.

Important Tip: Keep a file of all the notes and forms used in the interviews for both those selected and those not chosen. You may be glad to have this should someone challenge you, even legally, why they were not selected.

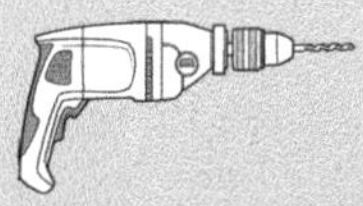

Application Ideas

1. Create an interviewing form like the one shown above, with scales for both the quality of the answer and the quality/confidence of the response.

2. Create a standard operating procedure (SOP) for conducting all future job interviews. Pass it through your HR and legal departments for review if possible. *Be sure all the questions are fair and legal.* Train all managers on how to conduct great interviews.

TOOL NUMBER THREE

Onboarding

Engaging Folks from the Start

Earlier in the book in the chapter on enrolling, I introduced the importance of onboarding by sharing the story of my daughter and my experiences with soldiers in the Army.

Onboarding is simply the process of getting people excited and "enrolled" in the first few days of joining your team. There is a rather narrow window of time to properly onboard from the moment a new hire or transfer arrives bright-eyed and bushy-tailed on the first day on the job. You want them to instantly feel welcome, supported, and ready to engage.

I once saw a darling poster of a tiny kitten with the words, "Things are often at their best in the beginning." This can be true when people are brought aboard. What you do in the first hours and days can make all the difference.

We will now put our selves into the shoes of Sarah, who was recently hired onto your team or perhaps has joined your team in an organization. (You have undoubtedly experienced the myriad of emotions when you first open the door and enter your new job environment where you could potentially spend months and years.)

For simplicity, I would like to suggest some things to do in the first 24 hours, 36 hours, and 10 days of someone's arrival to your team. Note: these time frames are not set in stone but should be closely followed.

On the first day:

Ok, Sarah, it's the first day! (Here is how to set the stage for her the moment she arrives.)

1. She is warmly welcomed by her manager and coworkers. Hopefully, they stand to greet her.
2. She has all her physical spaces cleaned and organized. She is given a desk, stapler, post-it notes, and anything else standard to a good workspace.
3. "Welcome Sarah" balloons are on her desk (optional but so cool!).
4. Her computer, email, passwords, etc., are set up, working, and instantly available to her when she sits down.
5. A stack of business cards is on her desk. The business cards have her name, position, and all contact information on the front, and on the back is the company mission statement. It will be fun for her to take business cards home that very day! Note: if it takes time to have official business cards finished, simply make ten temporary ones using Avery business card printable stock (Avery 5371).
6. Now, someone, preferably her direct manager, takes her on a walking tour of the building, facility, restrooms, break room, conference room, or any other relevant locations.
7. If possible, introduce her to her management chain: first and second level for sure and hopefully even the CEO or division chief.
8. Consider a welcome lunch where she can meet all her coworkers.

Within three days:

1. If not done already, sit her down and go over the company's mission, vision, values, measures of success and code of conduct down to her team level. Ask her why this mission excites her and how she feels her talents will contribute.
2. Make sure all-important personnel introductions have been made if they were not on the first day. Do not let this go longer!

3. Give her something meaningful to contribute immediately within the first week. Let her shine! Perhaps give her a problem to think about or solve.

4. Consider having her complete the 200 Talents Inventory page (available on our website in the store/tools section.) Go over it with her and ask her how she thinks her talents can best be put to maximum effectiveness. Ask her which talents she would like to learn or improve on while she is with you.

Within ten days:

There is a common "Ten Day Rule" when enrolling people to a team, especially in the Army. Studies have found that you have a maximum of ten days to get a new arrival fully acclimated, informed, and engaged with the team's vision, mission, and values. You also have that same amount of time to get them actively contributing in some important and unique way. You want them to really feel more than acclimated: they need to feel like themselves and see themselves as an active, unique contributor.

In the military, they found that if a soldier, sailor, or airman does not feel this in the first ten days, they maybe become victims of the "barracks rats" who are hoping to attract new "rats" to their nest of unmotivated, bad-mouthing, and basic non-performers.

Such barracks rats are not unique to the military: almost every organization has about ten percent of people who almost actively or perhaps subconsciously work against the morale, purpose, and success of the team. It might be their attitude that drives behavior, which can further affect the negative attitude, and unfortunately, this attitude virus can be contagious.

Most people want to belong. If they can't belong in a positive way, they may decide to belong in some other way. A blunt but sad statement is, "Some people would rather be wanted for murder than not wanted at all."

So, here's how we can help Sarah within her first ten days:

1. Get her on a project team that will enable her to use her talents and creativity to the fullest. This will help her feel the joy of contributing to a worthwhile project. Referring to her list of 200 Talents may help you choose the right position for her.

2. Help her go deeper into the one-to-three-year strategic plan of the organization. You want her to see she is part of a progressive organization with a great future for her, and you want her thoughts on the strategic plan.

3. Give her a sticky problem to be solved that requires some creativity and might require her to go out and gather information.

4. Arrange some "face time" with the CEO or most senior leader. This gives both an opportunity to meet each other informally and for the leader to get any ideas or impressions the new arrival may already have.

5. Remember that some studies show that, in many cases, the most revolutionary ideas in teams have come from people who have been there less than a few months and sometimes within just a couple of weeks. They have not been on board to become part of the furniture and only seeing and doing the things that are standard.

Imagine how excited Sarah is now that she feels fully engaged in the team. She knows the key people from the top down. She has a fully functional workstation and the ability to clearly communicate. She understands the values, mission, and basic strategy of the company or team. She has already put her fingerprint somewhere on something substantial where she can see her contribution in play.

And she is mentally, emotionally, physically, and even spiritually on board!

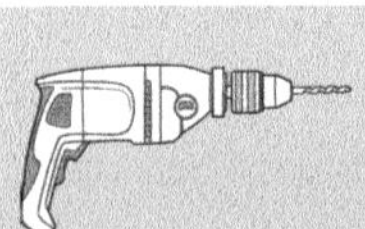

Application Ideas

1. Create a concrete action plan for onboarding new people based on the suggestions above and others you can think of.

2. Interview people who recently joined the team and inquire how they felt their on-boarding went. Ask them what could have been done differently to help them feel engaged and onboard.

3. Create an action team to create an onboarding plan and perhaps even a welcoming team to take the lead when someone new comes onboard.

TOOL NUMBER FOUR

Leading Inspiring Meetings!

The Power of Meetings: Do they *ZAP* or *SAP?*

"The two biggest problems in America are making ends meet and making meetings end."

Jokes abound about the misery of attending meetings, and the misery is often true. It is frustrating and disengaging to feel almost trapped in a seemingly endless meeting as people talk on and on and bring in items that were never on the agenda (if there even was one)!

(Perhaps worse, you are sitting in a meeting and realizing you had no real purpose to be there, and none of the discussed items have any pertinence to you.)

In a Dilbert cartoon, Dilbert is sitting back, disengaged, and remarks, "Only one hour of UBR to go!" UBR meaning Unfocused Boss Rambling.

Meetings are an extremely costly way to do business. If you multiply the value of the salary and benefits per hour times the number of hours in the meeting, the cost can be several thousand dollars. That is not counting the possible lack of production by their team while they are in the meeting. "I need a decision from the boss . . . Where is she?" "In a meeting all morning."

Yet meetings are an extremely critical part of team success because they can affect how people work for days and weeks to come.

When taking the helm, leaders need to master how to lead effective meetings. Effective meetings can accomplish in 45 minutes what might have taken hours before. Meetings give people critical face-to-face time where body language and other non-verbal communication are essential.

Being an effective meeting leader is a skill that people will greatly appreciate. So, let's learn how!

First, make sure that there is a valid and important reason to have a meeting and that there is no viable alternative. Boyd K. Packer, a prominent religious leader, once said, "It takes a mighty fine meeting to beat no meeting at all."

Once, I visited the headquarters of a client. In the main hallway, a large bright green wooden disk about six inches in diameter was hanging on a hook. My client told me a green disk means the meeting is on, but if it was flipped over to bright red on the other side, it meant there was no meeting today. But a red disk was also a signal and a directive for everyone to head *immediately* to their desk or phone and read the email that had been sent out. They had to promptly reply that they read the email with any needed responses. He made it clear that he would start holding mandatory meetings if his secretary did not get a 100% reply by nine o'clock. Very motivational!

There are effective alternatives to having meetings. If the only purpose of the meeting is to put out general information, perhaps a mandatory-read email or quick conference call will suffice.

When a meeting is necessary, put the central purpose of the meeting in the invitational email or text so people come prepared having thought about the issues.

Tip: Regarding emails, I learned a good tip from a client. Begin the subject line of nearly every internal email with an *A, B, C,* or *D.* This signals how important the email is. *A* means "open and read immediately." *B* means "read by the end of the day." *C* means "read by the end of the week," and *D* means that reading it is totally optional (or delete it because it is optional). This technique respects people's time and energy and helps avoid interrupting them as they work.

Second, invite the right people to a meeting. Invite only those whose presence is critical and who can provide important insights or decisions about the topic. (It is extremely frustrating for people to sit in a meeting knowing they really have no viable reason for being there.)

I previously cited the story of the egotistical U.S. Army Europe commander in Germany who spent hundreds of thousands of dollars bringing in a hundred people to his maintenance reporting meeting, mainly to show off his ego and superiority. This is what we want to avoid.

One way to respect people's time is to organize your meeting into a "peel-off" meeting. The first agenda items are important to everyone, and then you invite others to peel off and leave the meeting for the remaining agenda items unless they are interested. The only ones remaining are those who need to be there to the end.

Third, create the setting. The way you position chairs in the room can determine how people interact. Consider having water, treats, or coffee if one of the purposes is relaxed networking and socialization.

If you want to keep the meeting short, have a meeting standing up. I was surprised one time to be invited to a military meeting by a major general. When I arrived in the room, there were no chairs, and he was standing. We knew then the meeting would be short and to the point!

Fourth, and perhaps the most important, you cannot run an effective meeting without an agenda and a parking lot.

The Agenda: The agenda should include what each topic or item is, who will be presenting it, and the amount of time allocated to it. You may download a soft copy in the tool section of our website. Notice that the sample agenda includes the mission statement in the header at the top. (Everything in the meeting should relate somehow to the mission or purpose and you can even begin some meetings by having everyone recite it.)

Also, at the bottom of the template is a place for everyone to record any action assigned to them in a table that spells out who does what, when it should be done, and how they should follow up.

The Parking Lot: Obtain a dry-erase board that can be carried into any meeting. This is the "parking lot." Assign a parking lot attendant as one of the roles in the meeting. Whenever something that is not on the agenda comes up, it is written in the parking lot—what the item is, who brought it up, and the date it was brought up.

People quickly learn if they want it covered in the meeting, they need to get it on the agenda, or it will likely end up in the parking lot. If something is extremely important but not on the agenda, you may move something from the agenda to the parking lot and swap the new item in its place. *But never or rarely let the meeting go long!*

In the future, go to the parking lot to help create the next agenda. Add in the items that are still pertinent and unsolved. The parking lot can be shared electronically in a remote meeting.

Fifth, assign and rotate several roles in the meeting as follows:

The Meeting Leader: The meeting leader is the person responsible for leading the meeting. This does not always have to be the senior manager—in fact, it is very important to rotate who conducts the meeting. It energizes people and trains them. (This requires meeting with the boss ahead of time to understand the objectives.)

The Timekeeper: This person typically sits near the meeting leader, and it is their responsibility to make sure the agenda stays on track time wise. It is almost impossible for the meeting leader to lead the meeting and keep track of time. The timekeeper uses signals to tell people and the leader when the allocated time is up for a particular topic. If it turns out that more time is needed, something less critical can be moved to the parking lot in its place.

Action Catcher: This may be one of the most important roles in a meeting. An action catcher's job is to capture any direct or implied task by ensuring that the important information is clearly captured. They should know who is doing what, when the task should be accomplished, and how the teams are planning on following up. No one should leave the meeting without a clear understanding of every outcome or task and who it belongs to. *One task, one owner.*

The action catcher should be the last person to stand up or present at the end of the meeting. They go over every single task or assignment that came out of the meeting and make sure that it is perfectly clear **who is doing what, by when, and how they will be following up.**

Parking Lot Attendant: This person manages the parking lot as previously stated.

The Process Observer: This person keeps an eye on the dynamics of the meeting and makes sure participation is free and balanced and that people who have a comment are not ignored. (Sometimes meetings can be dominated by eager or talkative "spring-butts.")

Minute Keeper: this person keeps minutes of the meeting and creates the follow-up email. Sometimes, this role might be relatively permanent to a full-time assistant or secretary, where the other roles can rotate.

Logistician: This person is responsible for the logistics of the meeting, which might include setting it up or obtaining refreshments. (This position can also be part of the role of the minute keeper.)

I recommend that these roles be rotated and assigned in the meeting invitation so people can be mentally prepared ahead of time. You can even include them in the footer of the agenda.

IMPORTANT TIP!

Tip: It is extremely rude for anyone to be late to a meeting, especially causing the meeting to be delayed. This is particularly true if the senior manager or meeting leader is late. Here is a fun and simple way to motivate people to meet on time. Set some nice treats out ahead of time, *but only for those who arrive on time.* The meeting logistician removes the treats when the meeting is to start and replaces them with a "fine can." Anyone who is late must put a dollar bill or an IOU into the can. It is not much money, but it reinforces the right behavior. I once saw this in action, and people, even senior leaders, were literally running down the hall to be on time so as not to be fined! The collective fines can be donated or used to purchase treats for future meetings. *Smart!*

Finally, on to the ground rules. These are rules agreed upon by the whole group that drive meeting behavior. There should be no more than seven to ten. They may even be included in the footer of each meeting agenda. Here are some sample ground rules:

- We start and end meetings on time.
- We follow our agenda and use the parking lot.
- We keep our comments short and on target.
- We do not dominate or control the meeting.
- We pay a fun fine if we are late.
- We come to meetings on time and prepared.
- We agree to "love it for a minute."
- We do not interrupt others while they are contributing.

As mentioned in the book previously, I learned the *"love it for a minute"* from a client. Rather than firehose an idea or suggestion, the group agrees to love it for a minute: look at it respectfully and openly for how it might work before dismissing it.

In summary, I promise that if you follow the general guidelines, meetings can be short, powerful, focused, and effective. People can leave each meeting empowered, motivated, excited, and engaged.

But every ship has its difficult crew members, which we will address in the next tool, so read on!

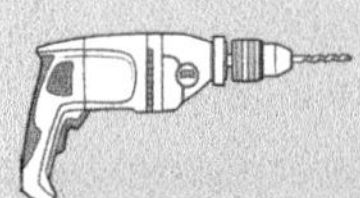

Application Ideas

1. Work with your team to develop meeting ground rules and get everyone's supporting vote or buy in.
2. Create a fun One Dollar Fine Bucket for latecomers and sometimes a treat prize for those who come on time.
3. Create a list of roles for people to play in the meeting and rotate those each meeting.
4. Create a standard agenda form for each meeting and put the mission statement at the top and ground rules at the bottom. You can download a sample from the tools section on www.VisionBound.com.

TOOL NUMBER FIVE

Working with Difficult Crewmembers

The theme of this book is based on the ship analogy, and it would be wonderful if all your crew members were delightful souls who cooperate and get along famously with each other and with your customers.

But this is rarely the case. You probably know who they are: the often or sometimes difficult, cantankerous, non-team members who drain the emotional and even physical energy of those around them.

My purpose is to give you just a few practical tools for working with these crew members. But remember, I previously mentioned my "fix or fire" rule: there is a limit to which you and your team must put up with clearly abhorrent, dysfunctional behavior. I have taught workshops on how to work with difficult people. I would like to summarize some ideas here.

Many years ago, I read a statement by a renowned religious leader who said the following:

> Jesus saw sin as wrong but also was able to see sin *as springing from deep and unmet needs* on the part of the sinner. This permitted Him to condemn the sin without condemning the individual. We can show forth our love for others even when we are called upon to correct them. We need

> to be able to look deeply enough into the lives of others to see the *basic causes* for their failures and shortcomings.
> —Spencer W. Kimball from "Jesus the Perfect Leader."

Though he used the word *sin*, I believe the same thing can be broadened to apply to any shortcoming or misbehavior we might see in ourselves or those around us. *Most of these can be traced back to unmet needs.*

I created this concept model of a tree having fruits and roots. The fruits, in this case, would be those behaviors in ourselves and others that fall short of what we would like to see and what those around us do not deserve. The deeper roots are those unmet needs that can result in less-desirable fruits.

I see four main roots: physical, mental, emotional, and spiritual. Each of these has a place in any team, workplace, individual, and family. Great leaders are in touch with and aware of how the team's culture is creating unmet needs in these areas. Mentally, people need challenge, stimulation, and mental growth. Emotionally, people need emotional safety, belonging, support, and love. Physically, people thrive when their physical needs are met in rest, nutrition, stress management, and hydration. Spiritually does not just have a religious connotation, but, in this case, it can simply mean a sense of deeper meaning and purpose in their lives and in their work. This traces back to Chapters Three and Five on the power of culture and creating vision and mission.

In my personal life, those around me, such as my wife of over forty-five years, know when I have PMS—pre-meal syndrome or what some call being "hangry." If I am hungry or dehydrated, my behaviors change. As parents of four children, we learned that getting a child to have a good, restful night's sleep led to an almost changed behavior or personality in the morning! Rest was their unmet need. Lecturing them about their behavior was the wrong thing to do.

Great leaders, parents, and co-workers can look for signs of these things and not harshly judge. COVID and other external, perhaps frightening conditions can lead to emotional and even physical danger. Lecturing or blaming people for their behaviors can only make it worse.

Leaders, including parents, can set the example of living more balanced lives. They may educate others on how to fill the unmet needs. Yet often when I visit client workplaces, I see the opposite: break rooms filled with caffeine laden coffees, sodas, and sugary snacks—the opposite of what people might need. Great leaders can also create work cultures that encourage and develop the four areas.

Physical

- Drink at least 64 ounces of water a day (eight 8-oz. glasses).
- Exercise three times a week for at least 30 minutes.
- Join a fitness club or work out with friends.
- Eat healthier meals.
- Listen to uplifting, relaxing music for 30 minutes a day.
- Get up in plenty of time, and don't be rushed.
- Take a nutrition class and practice what you learn.
- Cut down on or eliminate sodas, alcohol, and caffeine.
- Take a nice walk for half an hour a day.
- Swim at lunchtime.
- Learn or practice a sport every week.
- Take a fitness or exercise class.
- Start doing yoga or other stretching and relaxing activities.
- Get a workout app and start following it.
- Take time to look your very best every day.
- Grow a garden: it is great exercise!
- Play active games or sports with a friend or loved one.

Mental

- Take a class in a subject you are interested in.
- Read a good book for half an hour a day.
- Learn a new skill or language.
- Take up a stimulating hobby or craft.
- Take time to stop and ponder for fifteen minutes or more.
- Join a book club.

- Start a conversation with a new person each day.
- Make a new acquaintance every day.
- Renew one old friendship each week.
- Read the paper or a news magazine every day.
- Listen to classical music (good for the brain).
- Take an art class.
- Watch more educational channels on TV or the internet.
- Attend concerts and artistic events.

Emotional

- Make a new friend every day or at least every week.
- Renew an old friendship.
- Keep a journal about the emotions you are experiencing.
- Talk about your feelings with others.
- Practice being a good listener (others will listen to you).
- Read books on emotional health.
- Practice positive self-talk.
- Be around positive, emotionally healthy people.
- Distance yourself from unhealthy, negative people.
- Serve others less fortunate than yourself.
- Volunteer to serve your community.
- Enjoy the companionship of pets.
- Take a walk or exercise with a friend or significant other.
- Grow a garden.

Spiritual

- Read uplifting literature for a few minutes each day.
- Spend more time in nature.
- Pray and read the scriptures if it's something you believe in.
- Listen to great music that uplifts the spirit.
- Deeply connect with significant others.
- Visit museums, especially art museums.
- Become a committed member of your religious community.
- Love and bond with a favorite pet.
- Draw, paint, or create art that is spiritually enriching.

As leaders many of the ideas above can be promoted in the workplace. I am always impressed when I visit places with uplifting activities and leaders or committees that create opportunities for people to engage together from bowling to pickleball to book groups. Let your people brainstorm what they most would like to see!

Another way to look at the tree model is to see three main roots: personality, situation, and processes:

Personality Root: In his book *Coping with Difficult People,* Richard H. Bramson notes that probably about ten percent of people have what we might call difficult personalities. These are the most challenging because they come from perhaps years of experience, even back to childhood, and people have formed personalities that even give them an identity and shape many behaviors.

These are the most difficult to change because they are the deepest. Bramson's book gives insights into what this entails. Another superb book is *Dealing with People You Can't Stand* by Dr. Rick Brinkman and Dr. Rick Kirschner. I found their book to be deeper and more insightful, though I would have chosen a less abrasive title!

Situation Root: Each of us can become situationally difficult, even if personality-wise we are ok! These situations can come up in our personal or family lives outside of work. When you see someone who usually is evenly balanced and pleasant suddenly change, assume that something in their life has situationally changed. It may be short-lived, such as pain, an injury, or an illness, or take a long time to recover from, such as the death of a loved one or an economic or home-life situation.

As leaders and peers, we can work to recognize when suddenly behaviors or attitudes change and work performance declines or when people become unpleasant or difficult to work with. The adage, "be curious, not furious" is good advice.

In the great books, *Crucial Conversations* and *Crucial Accountability,* the authors list more than several ways we can explore and diagnose the underlying situations and show people we care enough to help however we can.

Process Root: Here, there are no major problems with personality or situation, but something in your processes has become so frustrating that people literally or symbolically throw up their hands, exhibit negative behaviors, and recruit others in complaint sessions.

In some ways, this root may be easier to solve because we may have little influence on people's personalities or personal situations. But we can and should tackle any processes causing frustration and disengagement. Focus groups and customer or staff surveys can help you identify what cumbersome or archaic processes are causing disenchantment. Studies suggest that most staff stress and disengagement come from poor processes, not poor people.

In summary, if we understand these principles and tools, we may be able to work with and even heal some of the challenging crew members, family members, neighbors, and others. Be curious, not furious, and if possible, seek to uncover their deep issues or unmet needs. Then, do what you can to help.

Our next tool outlines ways to better understand, lead, communicate with, and motivate the different age generations.

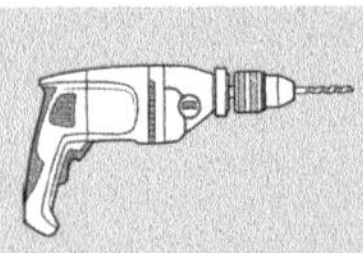

Application Ideas

1. Consider making a very private list of people who seem "difficult" and deeply think about the roots of possible unmet needs they might have.
2. Look at all the processes that might be causing frustrations, which lead to anger, resentment, gossiping, and other behaviors. Create problem-solving teams to find ways to improve those processes.
3. Create and distribute the list of physical, mental, emotional, and spiritual needs and consider having people privately assess themselves.
4. Create ways to better meet these needs in your team: clubs, walking or hiking groups, lessons on nutrition, more water and less soda, healthy snacks, etc.
5. Organize book groups or other special interest groups for people to join.
6. Download the unmet needs tree document from www.VisionBound.com

TOOL NUMBER SIX

Leading and Motivating the Different Generations

In this tool, we will explore a few differences manifest in the four or five generations that show up in our ship's crew manifest, focused on Traditionals, Baby Boomers, Gen X, and Gen Y/ Millennials.

Generally:

- If you were born before 1943, you are a **Traditional.**
- If you were born between 1944 and 1964, you are a **Baby Boomer.**
- If you were born between 1965 and 1981, you are **Generation X.**
- If you were born between 1982 and 2003, you are a **Millennial/Generation Y.**

There are sub-sets called **cuspers**, sandwiched between the generations. They share characteristics of the main generations before them and after them.

- 1940–1945 (between Traditionals and Baby Boomers)
- 1962–1967 (between Baby Boomers and Generation X)
- 1978–1983 (between Generation X and Millennials)

Here is a short summary of ways you, as a leader, can understand, connect to, and motivate the four generations. Some of this information is derived and modified from the outstanding book,

Sticking Points by Hayden Shaw.

Traditionals

Shaped by: the Great Depression, World War II, the Korean War, and the Red Scare.

Modus operandi and products: the automobile, formal letters, and home ownership. Jobs are often for life. Often disengaged from technology or are new to it. Duty, honor, and country.

Characterized by:

- feeling needed in the workplace
- having financial security
- believing in duty before pleasure

Behaviors: Traditionals are much more loyal to employers and thus are more disciplined and consistent in the workplace. They may be shocked and incensed if someone who has worked for your company for less time is promoted, as they expect to be promoted from job tenure.

As team players, they are used to and most comfortable working as a team in a well-defined chain of command. The boss decides. They process information mainly in print and rely on experts. They now want to slow down a bit. They typically communicate by writing memos, sending letters, listening to speeches, and calling meetings. "I give respect by figuring out the hierarchy and finding my place in it."

Their theme might be "Do what I have to do to give my family a better life." or "Always faithful."

1. Reinforce that they have a secure position with your company.

2. Give them a sense of loyalty and support from you and other top leaders.

3. Take time to develop them and build the skills necessary to help them survive long-term in today's workplace.

4. Have them share life experiences and lessons. They often are very wise, and it shows deep respect that you want to learn from them and about them.

Baby Boomers

Shaped by: the Vietnam War, the 60's culture, the moon landings, rebellion, the civil rights movement, John F. Kennedy's death, and nuclear families.

Modus operandi and products: the television and the telephone. High achievers. They want job security. Careers are defined by employers. Early adopters of technology. Seek status, advancement, and work success and will sacrifice self and family for work. Motivate with traditional HR offerings.

As individuals, they like to "do my own work." Comfortable with both print and electronics and find entertainers compelling. They want to use decision-making processes, but the boss ultimately decides. Often sandwiched between taking care of parents and children, trying to figure out how to make it all work. They often write memos, pick up the phone, and set up appointments. "I can work my way up to a position that gets respect."

Characterized by:

- working long hours
- needing personal gratification and individual choice
- wanting status/position that displays their success

Behaviors: Baby Boomers tend to be more confident in taking on new tasks if they're allowed to do things their way, and often measure a team's work ethic depending on the hours worked. They are not as formal in the workplace as Traditionals but they do expect a degree of formality. They want to grow, have long-term opportunities, move up, and find satisfaction in moving up.

Their theme might be "Work hard and get ahead."

1. Give them more money, a bonus, or a raise.
2. Provide them with a position with a strong title as they move up within the company.
3. Give them more challenges to utilize their creativity so they don't get bored.

Generation X

Shaped by: music changes, CDs, the world "shrinking," the AIDS crisis, globalization, 9/11.

Modus operandi and products: personal computers and email. They seek work-life balance. Digital immigrants. Clever, resourceful, anti-corporate. Loyal to a profession but not necessarily employers. Self-reliant risk-takers and good team players. Whoever is the savviest on the subject should make the decision, not necessarily the boss. Skeptical about authority. Contributing is more important than tenure and compensation is more than benefits. They typically want non-monetary benefits, control over work schedules, project credit, and increased responsibility.

Characterized by:

- needing emotional security and positive reinforcement
- wanting a casual and fun work environment
- desiring flexibility between work and life

Behaviors: Generation X are more informal in the workplace. Typically, they are independent workers who value work as a place to grow personally and professionally. As individuals, they want to do what needs to be done in the fastest and most efficient way. They want to enjoy life more now, not just when they retire.

They want opportunities to grow, learn, and enhance their skills now. Print is less important to them, and they prefer digital, email, and the World Wide Web. But they are also feeling the squeeze of caring for Baby Boomer parents who are nearing retiring and having children of their own. "I will give you respect if you prove to me that you deserve it."

Their theme might be "Work as hard as I have to in order to get a life."

1. Give them recognition and praise more often.
2. Provide them with a flexible schedule.
3. Give them opportunities to learn and grow.

Millennials / Generation Y

Shaped by: 9/11, loss of societal safety, Desert Storm/Shield, the fall of the Berlin Wall, the explosion of technology and social media, political rancor, and a loss of trust in the government.

Modus operandi and products: Smart Phones, texting, social media. Prize freedom and flexibility. Digital natives. Work *with* not *for* organizations. More independent but enjoy teams. Less interested in home ownership and more motivated by free time, sports, hobbies. Like frequent feedback. Easily distracted and find it harder to focus if work is not rewarding and interesting. Frequent job-hoppers.

Characterized by:

- having an entrepreneurial spirit with a need to start movements
- wanting instant gratification
- having an "everybody wins" attitude

Behaviors: Millenials are very entrepreneurial and can be very concerned about helping a community start a movement. Their self-expression is more important than self-control. A sense of accomplishment is very important to them, so they will be very dedicated to you for helping them achieve their goals. They are more team players than Gen X but want to differentiate themselves in the team.

Instant messaging and social networking emerged as major sources of information, and Millenials may not even read what is sent to them in print. They are looking for ways to express their talents and interests at work. As far as decision making, they like to work through the options and decide together, and if they can't, let the boss decide. They don't want to feel like they are working all the time like their parents and grandparents did, then try to make it all up on yearly vacations! "I will give respect to those who get it and will take me seriously."

Their theme might be "Work but make a difference."

1. Give them a greater sense of purpose beyond the organization (volunteer opportunities).
2. Provide them with ways to win almost daily (company/personal goals).
3. Use up-to-date technology to train them and help them be more successful (webinars, podcasts, etc.).
4. Invite them to use their tech skills to do research and problem-solving. Giving them a challenge that lets them use their technology skills and smartphones is very motivating and engaging!

Also, they appreciate flexible work schedules, less formal dress standards, and a fun work environment.

Summary: We can learn tools to leverage the uniqueness and power of the various generations, both at work and in our personal relationships. Understanding and appreciating these differences also builds trust and helps with all the handles of our Helm Model.

We can now transition to the next tool, which outlines the differences between the two main genders in life and in the workplace and how to respect and leverage these differences.

Application Ideas

1. Consider all the people in your life, whether at work or in your personal life. Perhaps make a list of them and what generation they fall into.
2. Discuss with some of them and see if they agree with the characterizations in this workbook.
3. Work on ideas on how to relate to and how to envision, enroll, empower, and engage them.

TOOL NUMBER SEVEN

Understanding and Leading the Two Main Genders

You don't have to live very long before you realize there are large differences between boys and girls and men and women. Effective leaders, parents, families, and community members understand the differences enough to skillfully lead both men and women.

The subject is too vast to address here, so I refer you to the excellent book *Talking Nine to Five* by Dr. Deborah Tannen. She is one of the best authors on this topic and has written numerous and well-researched books and articles.

Much of my interest in this subject came from Dr. John Gray's famous and early books, *Men are From Mars and Women are from Venus*. I listed other books on this subject in my book list found later in the book.

This section summarizes some findings and research in this area of men and women in communication and relationships. With the increasing involvement of transgender people, the issue becomes more complex and less black and white. Much research is emerging on the subject.

Physiological Differences in Brain Design

The understanding that men and women are fundamentally different in brain design is relatively new. Feminist Charlotte Perkins Gilman declared 100 years ago: "There is no female mind. The brain is not an organ of sex. You might as well speak of a female liver."

In fact, one of the biggest revolutions in the study of brain anatomy is the growing acknowledgment that few organs are as sexually dimorphic (different) as the human brain. One difference is the corpus callosum (the part of the brain that connects the right and left sides). The corpus callosum and the two connecting cables, the anterior commissure and the massa intermedia, are larger in women, allowing more cross-lateral connections in the brain.

Researchers at Cambridge University further collaborated with Stanford and the University of Pennsylvania, completed an exhaustive study of the past 20 years of male/female brain design. They looked at over 160 research studies and identified over 100 differences, including:

- **Grey matter/white matter differences.** Gray matter represents information processing centers in the brain, and white matter represents the networking of, or connections between, these processing centers. In general, men have approximately 6.5 times the amount of gray matter than women, and women have nearly ten times the amount of white matter than men. Their brain design naturally moves women toward relationship issues.

According to Rex Jung, a UNM neuropsychologist and co-author of the study, this may help to explain why men tend to excel in tasks requiring more local processing (like mathematics). In contrast, women tend to excel at integrating and assimilating information from distributed gray matter regions in the brain, such as those required for language facility.

The study also identified regional differences in intelligence. For example, 84 percent of gray-matter regions and 86 percent of white-matter regions involved with intellectual performance in women were found in the brain's frontal lobes, compared to 45 percent and zero percent for males, respectively. The gray matter driving male intellectual performance is distributed throughout more of the brain.

Dr. Daniel Amen's SPECT brain scans show that entirely different areas of male and female brains light up under similar stimuli or scenarios. *Interestingly, the area of the brain with common sense hardly registers with men when presented with a crazy or dangerous "manly man" challenge.* This may explain why men gravitate to doing crazy things that women would not even think of! (Famous last words of some men: "Hey, buddy, hold my beer and watch this!")

Thus, men and women are thinking with fundamentally different organs. This helps explain some of the information I outline below.

That said, keep in mind that there are many other factors affecting gender differences, ranging from birth order to upbringing and culture and a myriad of other reasons. Also, you may find that, despite your gender, you are completely the opposite of these general findings. Others at work or in your family may also be different from these generalizations.

Bottom Line Up Front (BLUF)

- *Men:* "report talk" on information and activities as a sort of bonding. *Women:* "rapport talk" on problems and relationships. When women try rapport talk with men, it often makes men uncomfortable.
- *Men* tease to create status or male bonding. *Women* compliment (and sometimes tease) to connect and be friendly.
- *Men* give orders more directly. Women give orders more indirectly.
- *Men* are goal-oriented, dislike processes, and view things through power lenses. *Women* are more process-oriented and view things through relationship lenses.
- *Men* move off emotional ground quickly and into action to divert this energy whereas *women* want to stay in the emotional energy to resolve it.

More Details

Men

- Work is played by rules of power.
- The goal is to keep *power differentiated.*

- Men are very aware of the power structure and hierarchy and seek to maintain it by the rules.
- The primary purpose of work is economic, self-gratification, and self-promotion.
- "Take the dog out" or "Turn the heat up."

Women

- Work is played by rules of *relationships.*
- The goal is to keep power dead-even and may even attack other women for violating the dead-even rule in getting promoted.
- If they have a home business, a significant purpose of it will be to make friends and have warm working relationships.
- "The dog needs to go out" or "It's getting cold in here."

Men

- Look through a *competition* lens.
- They emphasize how they are different from other men.
- They keep power differentiated and behave correctly according to place in the hierarchy.

Women

- Look through a *connection* lens.
- They emphasize how they are similar to other women.
- They view things in a flat structure, seeking win-win situations.
- They don't usually care about power.

Men

- Focus on goals.
- They get confused by all the process or relationship issues.
- They can get things done through men or women with just orders and little process.
- They may interpret tasks as optional if they are buried in a bunch of processes.

Women

- Focus on process.
- They expect process and relationship-based work. They must do more process work to get things done through other women.
- Shopping vs. hunting analogy: men go to "buy" and women go to "shop."

Men

- "Report talk": They talk about things, objects, and activities, focusing on details and statistics.
- Men may feel uncomfortable by inquiries into health or other personal problems as they take it as a one-down to them or a question of their virility or problem-solving abilities!

Women

- "Rapport talk": They talk about problems as a way to connect with others.
- Women express concern about health as a genuine desire to connect and care. Many women are more in-tune with their bodies and expressive about how they physically feel. Again, it is a connector for them to talk about health issues and inquire about them to connect.

Men

- They try to do their best by solving problems quickly and are then hurt when women get mad for them doing it.

Women

- Women present problems as devices to connect and present problems and process discussions as connectors and get mad when men try to just quickly "kill" the problem with a solution.
- They solve problems more slowly, ensuring power is even, and others are validated. They view problems as opportunities to bond and connect.

Men

- Men give you the bottom line and back-fill the process only if needed or asked.
- They are often clueless to meta-messages and non-verbals.

Women

- Women take you through the process and then give you the bottom line.
- They are more aware of meta-messages and acutely aware of non-verbals.

Men

- Men make quick decisions and issue orders.
- They are more comfortable with unilateral decisions and feel oppressed by lengthy discussions about minor decisions.

Women

- Women expect decisions to be discussed first and then made by consensus.
- Women use lengthier discussions as opportunities to communicate and bond.

Men

- Men can do one thing or another in a focused way.
- As bosses, men admire and promote others who are focused and single-tasked (men's brains are hard-wired for single-tasking).

Women

- Women can do multiple things simultaneously.
- As bosses, women want men to multitask! Note that the female brain is physiologically hard-wired for multitasking by having a larger corpus callosum connecting the brain's hemispheres and allowing more connections.

Men

- Learn to face conflict.
- They look for win-lose outcomes to preserve power and status. They are geared to a winner-takes-all mentality.

Women

- Learn to avoid conflict.
- They look for win-win outcomes.
- They are geared for doing what is good and fair for all.
- They do not like conflict and opposition because they see it as injurious to the relationship.

Men

- They use oppositional stance/ritual opposition to explore ideas and play the devil's advocate to point out potential flaws in reasoning. (This can even be a sign of acceptance and respect because they want to bond with you as a worthy opponent in their sport of problem-solving).
- They may not take opposition as seriously and view it more as a game.
- When the game is over, it's over!

Women

- Women may take opposition literally and may feel personally attacked.
- The game is *never* or *rarely* over.

Men

- Men may view questions as a game to be hunted and killed.
- They want to kill questions quickly one by one.
- They may feel interrogated by women's questions.

Women

- Women may use questions as a medium for discussion or connectedness.
- Women want to connect through their questioning. They are not trying to interrogate or challenge the man!

Men

- Men may make things up rather than admit they don't know.
- They rarely apologize, even when they are wrong.

Women

- Women don't hesitate to say they don't know. They tend to be more honest in this area.
- They use ritual apologies frequently as smoothers in a conversation.
- This is often a problem for women. They apologize even when they have done nothing wrong, and this can make them appear less professional.

Men

- Men tend to like verbal bantering.
- They tease each other as male bonding. They tease for fun to play on status and rarely compliment other men. For example, my wife and I sometimes meet with our very long-time friends, Jim and Barbara. I would say to Jim, "Hey, putting on a little weight now, huh?" and he would reply, "Yeah, take a look in a mirror!" I can't image my wife saying that to Barbara!

Women

- Women tend to dislike verbal bantering and teasing.
- They use compliments and expect compliments as bonding tools instead.

Men

- Friendships come and go, and they tend to take things less personally.
- They resist being influenced in public.

Women

- Friendship runs deeper, and they take things more personally.
- They give up the floor to men and are more willing to seem influenced to keep power even and make others feel good (even though they may be stubbornly resisting inside!).

Men

- They tend to be lengthy in meetings (to appear in charge and important) but give fewer reports back.
- They set things up physically to enforce position or power.

Women

- They tend to be brief in their comments in meetings (they share the time with others). Report back on events with details of what, why, when, and who.
- They set the room up to promote communication and relationships.

Men

- They don't question goal lines.
- "I'll fix it if it kills me." "Trust me."

I love the quote, "Never let a problem to be solved become more important than a person to be loved" (Thomas S. Monson).

Women

- They think things are up for discussion!
- "I'll help you if it kills you." "Be nice."

There is great synergy when we respect and draw upon the differences between men and women in the workplace and our personal lives and families.

In summary, there are significant differences between men and women, from physiological or brain design to chemical and cultural differences.

Sometimes, we get needlessly frustrated and even angry when we attribute certain behaviors to an *individual* instead of seeing that these may be natural inclinations of their *gender* and the unique nature of their brains, chemicals, and social programming. I hope some of these ideas help you understand the complexity of men and women in communication, work, and personal relationships.

In the next tool, we turn to how to focus our organizational power on creating outstanding service cultures.

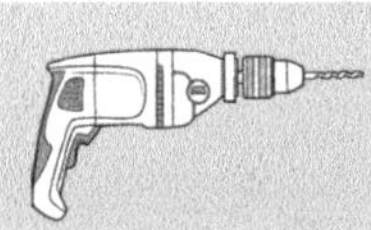

Application Ideas

1. Have a discussion with the men and women in your life and see if they generally agree with the data and characterizations listed in this section.
2. Contact us if you would like an assessment tool that you can use to lead these discussions.
3. Contact us if you want my wife and me to bring our workshop to your team or set up a survey to see how your team is like or not like some of these concepts. We can also deliver the workshop by webinar online.

TOOL NUMBER EIGHT

Building and Leading a True Service Culture

"The task of leadership is not to put greatness into people, but to elicit it. The greatness is already there."
—John Buchan, Canadian politician

I have long enjoyed this John Buchan quote about greatness. It not only applies to leadership but to life and people in general. It also applies to the topic of this section—how to build greatness into your service culture. Greatness is already in your people, the task is to elicit it, and put them in systems and processes that allow that greatness to flourish!

Leadership is a great force multiplier, and it certainly applies when building a world-class customer service program. Some of these following ideas are expanded in my book, *Customers Only Want Two Things: Winning Loyalty in a Competitive World.* It is available on Amazon.

This falling domino graphic provides an illustration. When someone pushes a very small, lightweight domino it tips and hits one slightly larger and heavier. That domino then tips and hits the bigger one behind it. The tumbling continues until a huge domino weighing over a hundred pounds and two feet high falls over. Videos of falling dominoes are fun to watch on YouTube.

Leadership often provides the initial motivation and energy which can multiply through the organization. (Sometimes, leaders block the process with micromanagement or other restraints, and the synergy stops cold.) After working with many companies and teams the world over in helping them reach new levels of customer service I have learned some ideas.

Here is a remarkable hero story shared by Valerie Oberle, vice president of Disney University Guest programs. She has told the story to audiences and shared it in the book *Chicken Soup for the Soul at Work.*

It seems a guest was checking out of Disney World's Polynesian Village Resort in Florida. She'd had a great time but told the front desk hostess she was heartbroken over losing some rolls of film, particularly the shots of the Polynesian Luau. The hostess asked her to leave a couple rolls of fresh film. Two weeks later, this guest received a package containing new photos of Disney World, including the parade, and shots of the entire cast of the Luau, personally autographed by the performers! These photos had been taken by the front desk hostess after work on her own time. (Of course, with our modern phones, taking and sharing such photos is much easier than it used to be!)

Valerie saw the thank-you letter this guest wrote to Disney, in which the submitter said that never in her life had she received such compassionate service from any business. For the complete story, see "Customer Service is not a Mickey Mouse Affair" in the book *Heart at Work*, page 113.

I was astonished by this story. That a front desk hostess, serving hundreds of people a day, would care enough to go that extra mile for one person is almost mind-boggling. Valerie said, "Heroic service does not come from policy manuals. It comes from people who care—and from a culture that encourages and models that attitude."

There is a gulf of difference between the "zeros" and the anonymous "heroes" at Disney World. Obviously, much can be attributed to the character of the individuals involved. However, I also attribute much of it to the force multiplier of leadership that created the culture and spirit that Valerie referred to.

A friend of mine shared another experience he had at Disneyland in California when he took his wife and six children there on a hot summer day. In the mid-afternoon, his two-year-old was hot and exhausted. The last straw was when she spilled her soda down her dress. She was bawling, the other children were upset, and all wondered what to do. It felt like the day was ruined. However, a cast member walking by saw the family in distress and walked over to see what she could do. Perhaps in her mind was Disney's mission: **create happiness.**

She took in the situation briefly, went into a nearby store on Main Street. She came out three minutes later with a brand-new pink Disney princess dress and a magic wand. She helped the mother dress the little girl, put the wand in her hand, and said, "That's better. Have a great day in the Magic Kingdom."

She smiled again and walked away, *never charging the family a dime.* However, the family walked away with their dancing princess and stayed at Disneyland for seven hours longer, including an expensive dinner! The husband told me, "Disneyland won my loyalty, and I will take my family back as often as I can."

What a return on investment for a dress and a wand, which cost Disneyland probably about twenty-five dollars in total.

I learned that, back then, Disney gave each staff member a dollar amount they could use, at their discretion, to instantly give visitors a great experience. That cast member did not have to run to a manager for approval nor fill out some form. She was trusted and empowered.

Is a Service Program a Hero or a Zero?

In my seminars, I sometimes stretch a ten-foot piece of paper across a wall and write "zero" at one end and "hero" at the other, with a one-to-ten scale between. I ask participants to place a check mark along the scale as if they were one of their company's customers being asked the Ultimate Question: *"How likely is it you would recommend our business to a friend or family member?"*

I usually see votes across the paper, with the most grouped in the 6-7 range. Will mere satisfaction (6–7) keep customers coming back again and again? Is it good enough to be world class? We need them in the 9–10 range (loyal!). Let us apply the force multipliers of leadership to cross this gulf.

(You can learn much more about the Ultimate Question in the fine book, *The Ultimate Question*, by Fred Reichheld.)

Don't forget the eNPS question from Chapter Thirteen: "*How likely is it you would recommend working for us to a friend or family member?*" If a team has a low eNPS, don't expect the staff to provide much better service to customers or even to each other. Managers are the single most important factor in creating this loyalty.

Renowned author Marcus Buckingham said, "People don't quit companies. They quit managers."

The Seven Force Multipliers of Customer Service Leadership

I propose that there are at least seven force multipliers that leaders can apply as they build a world-class customer service program. At the end of the chapter, you can use some questions to evaluate your own program.

Number One: The Power of a Compelling Vision

President Ronald Reagan once said, "*To grasp and hold a vision, to fix it in your senses, that is the very essence, I believe, of successful leadership.*" Great organizations, be it families, businesses, or nations, are focused on a compelling vision—a vision that ignites and unifies the hearts of all engaged in it. A vision that excites positive emotion when you read it and makes you want to live it.

Before manufacturing his first Model T car, Henry Ford began with the end in mind with a clear, concise vision: "I will build a car for the great multitude. It will be large enough for the family, but small enough for the individual to run and care for. It will be constructed of the best materials, by the best men to be hired, after the simplest designs that modern engineering can devise. But it will be low in price that no man making a good salary will be unable to own one and enjoy with his family the blessing of hours of pleasure in God's great open spaces."

Henry Ford's vision statement contains elements of an effective corporate vision and it is *concise, clear, compelling,* and *measurable.* It engages the hearts of those who read it. It provides a crystal-clear picture of what the end must be.

Most of all, it drove everything that Ford did in the early days. When the current process of building cars was too expensive to realize his vision, Henry challenged the process and refined the assembly line system to the point that Model T's were selling for less than $300.00. That is the power of a vision.

Dr. Stephen R. Covey said, "Leadership is the creation of a culture or a relationship surrounding a common vision." I propose that the original vision of Walt Disney, even though he is long dead, created the culture that helped inspire the front desk hostess to be such a hero that day. As I quoted before, Walt Disney said, "We will do what we do so well that the people who see it will want to see it again and bring friends." With tens of millions of visitors to some parks each year, Disney has often succeeded.

Great leaders unite their teams in a process called "co-missioning." Great visions and missions are best created when as many people as possible are involved in their inception. This process can also be called "pathfinding," which, more simply stated, is *linking what the folks out there are passionate about getting with what your organization and people are passionate about giving.* Disney applies the power of pathfinding in one of its early mission statements, *"We create happiness by providing the finest in entertainment to people of all ages everywhere."*

In just fifteen words, Disney created a compelling vision that not only tells "what" they do but, more importantly, "why." They link what they are passionate about giving (fine entertainment) with what their customers are passionate about getting: happiness.

The Walt Disney Company now has a much longer mission statement: "To entertain, inform and inspire people around the globe through the power of unparalleled storytelling, reflecting the iconic brands, creative minds and innovative technologies that make ours the world's premier entertainment company." (In my opinion, it is too long to be memorized or used by front-level staff.)

I have worked with dozens of organizations to help them create mission and vision statements that resonate like Disney's former one. Usually, mission statements are cumbersome, wordy, uninspiring, and completely forgettable. They are "framed whatever" stuck on a wall somewhere, gathering dust. I will share a couple of examples of how a mission statement can evolve.

I was working with a movie theater to help them create a compelling and exciting mission. Their previous mission statement was a "framed whatever" that read something like this:

"Our mission is to provide our customers with a positive movie-going experience by providing them with a clean theater, top-quality new-release movies and . . ." blah, blah, blah. (You've heard this stuff before, right?)

After a little work, they came up with one that was quite a bit better (or at least shorter).

"We guarantee top-quality movie-going experiences to our valued customers by providing superb recent-release movie entertainment in an uplifting, positive environment in the cleanest theater in the valley."

But it still does not connect what they are passionate about giving with what customers are passionate about getting. It is missing the critical "why" piece. We went back to work and created the final version:

"We provide refreshment for the soul by providing a complete movie experience in the finest theater in the valley.

We do this through:

- *maintaining the cleanest theater in the region,*
- *treating every customer like family,*
- *creating our friendly, family atmosphere,*
- *smiling at and personally greeting every patron,*
- *offering unique services, and*
- *remembering the little things are the big things."*

You can see and feel the difference. The final statement captures the deeper purpose of their mission and provides some specific ways to do it. By using the bullets beneath, they did not jumble up the main statement and kept it at 19 words.

My challenge for an organization is to create in ten or fifteen words or less a compelling mission that uplifts, excites, and unites every stakeholder who reads it. The bullets underneath can add detail.

My second example is even more insightful. I was working with a financial planning and financial services company in California. Their mission statement was a mumbo-jumbo lengthy mess of financial jargon about a half-page long. I kept drilling them to understand exactly what they offered their customers. Why do people hunger for financial services such as retirement planning, college savings, and insurance? In the end, we created a six-word statement that says it all: *"We let you sleep at night."*

This statement is more of a vision statement because it doesn't say anything about what they do. However, it was a great marketing slogan. In fact, they made billboards that just shone with those six words and their company name. To translate it into a mission statement, they might do this: *"We let you sleep at night by solving your financial concerns."*

"Our mission statement about treating people with respect and dignity is not just words but a creed we live by every day. You can't expect your employees to exceed the expectations of your customers if you don't exceed the employees' expectations of management."
—Howard Schultz, CEO Starbucks Coffee

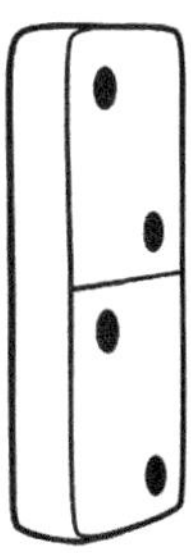

Number Two: The Power of Engagement

The most compelling and exciting mission statement in the world won't have much impact unless it is drilled deeply into a team's culture and the hearts, minds, and actions. Staff must be empowered and resourceful at all levels to bring it to life. Otherwise, it's only worth the paper it's printed on.

I heard once that Disney leaders were shocked to discover that the average 17-year-old job applicant at Disneyland did not even know that there was once a real person named Walt Disney, and they knew nothing about him, his dream, or what he created. After all, they were born long after the TV show *Disney's Wonderful World of Color*, hosted by Walt himself, was off the air.

This inspired Disney to create its famous orientation program where each employee learns about the history of Disney's dream and what the real values and purposes of Disney are. They are then "put in costume" and sent out to serve, even if it is as a street sweeper on Main Street. They know *their mission is to make people happy, not simply sweep the streets.* Once, a child of a friend of mine spilled her drink at Disney. A street sweeper saw it, asked what kind of drink it was, and brought her a new one. A vision in action!

My last example inspired my wife and me in a recent trip to Colonial Williamsburg. Its mission is to *Feed the human spirit by sharing America's enduring story.* As we walked its historic streets and interacted with the many colonial-costumed staff, we felt our spirits *were* deeply fed and instilled with a deeper love for America's truly enduring history.

So, once you have a vision, how do you engage everyone to bring it to pass? **First and foremost, communicate it and communicate it some more!** Have everyone memorize it.

1. Print it on the back of business cards (and give every employee business cards. It makes them feel they belong). Hint: Use perforated laser business cards and whip out cards as needed. Or use a low-cost, fast response printing company.
2. Put it on the header or footer of all internal memos, documents, and meeting agendas so it can be referred to in all deliberations.
3. Recite the vision or mission frequently.
4. Create a symbol to represent the mission.
5. Role-play how to live the mission. My daughter worked for a fast-food place that had the employees team up to create a skit, a song, and a battle cry around it. She still hasn't forgotten the statement!

Here are a few suggestions:

- Establish a dollar range mentioned in the Disney example.
- Train employees on how to satisfy a customer

problem in a way that wins loyalty. Remember, if you try to motivate people without training them, you only frustrate them!

- Establish a set of clear standards and guidance.
- Create a list of Frequently Asked Questions (FAQ) with their Frequently Given Responses (FGR) and thoroughly train every employee in how to use them.

"Whether you are big or small, you cannot give good customer service if your employees don't feel good about coming to work." —Martin Oliver, M.D. Kwik-Fit Financial Services

---

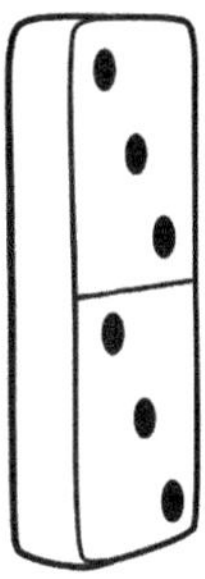

Number Three: Recognize and Reward Examples of Living the Mission

The adage, "You get what you reward," rings true in the service environment. Leaders can get in the habit of watching for instances where employees live the mission and deliver what it promises. To do this, they may have to symbolically grow two new eyeballs that only see the good things (their old eyeballs may be too well trained to see only the problems!)

Try to catch employees in doing things right and instantly recognize them. These recognitions need not be expensive. Simple gestures of specific, timely thanks and small things like candy or movie passes will often do the trick.

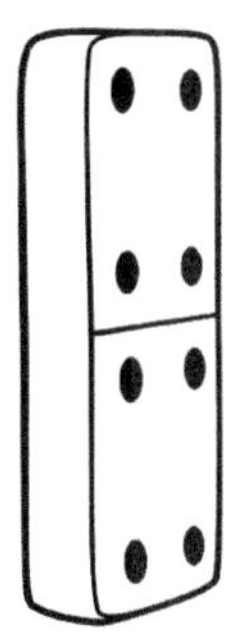

Number Four: Do More Leadership by Wandering Around (LBWA)

This is one of the most powerful tools I know of to become a more influential, engaged leader. It's easy to get so caught up in the whirlwind of the job that leaders get stuck behind their desks or off and running to meetings. Set aside a good half hour each day to LBWA: simply walk around visiting people and engaging with them on a personal basis. Never use this time to correct or find fault. Praise them for the work they are doing or past performance. Learn about their families, hobbies, and interests, and share yours with them. At times, you can ask some questions related to work.

A few good LBWA questions are:

7. How are you doing?
8. What are you learning?
9. What does the team need to learn?
10. What can I do differently to help you do your job better?
11. Is there something frustrating you about your job that I could be aware of?
12. What is something we can do differently as a team to better serve our customers?

"Spread love everywhere you go. Let no one ever come to you without leaving happier." –Mother Teresa, Roman Catholic nun and missionary

---

Other ideas include:

1. Involve customers in recognizing great service. One hotel gives each customer a gold coin to award an employee who does a particularly good job.

2. Have a peer-recognition program where peers can catch a fellow employee doing something well, submit a "gotcha card" and be recognized for doing so.

3. Create a unique pass-along award that can travel from employee to employee as they catch each other performing excellent service. I recently visited a university bookstore that created a SPAM award (Super Positive Attitude Master). They mounted a can of Spam on a trophy, created a SPAM T-shirt, and passed the trophy around to recognize great acts of service. Fantastic.

4. Read the book *A Thousand and One Ways to Reward Employees* by Bob Nelson for dozens of low-cost, innovative ways to reward others. Another great book is *The 24 Carrot Manager* by Adrian Gostick.

> When we treat people as objects, we dehumanize them.
> —Brene Brown, author and researcher

Remember: The Power of Onboarding the Right Folks

It's crucial to make the right hires. Almost every leader has made the mistake of hiring the wrong person, personality wise, into a service position. As mentioned previously, Southwest Airlines, famous for its friendly, energetic staff, has a simple credo: *Hire for personality and train for skill.*

One Target store manager told me he hired for the 3 F's: fast, fun, and friendly. He learned if people were fast, fun, and friendly, he could train them in virtually any retailing skill.

If the first two force multipliers are done well, finding and retaining good folks will be a lot easier. The Mirage Hotel has a long waiting list of people wanting to be on their housekeeping team because friends tell friends what it's like to work in a positive environment. Disney has no shortage of applicants who wish to work for a place that "makes people happy."

Nevertheless, a good hiring process must separate the likely top performers and deliver people with the right mix of personality, skill, and trainability to create a world-class service team. And it *must* involve behavior-based interviewing. Be sure to use a battery of interview questions to reveal a person's personality style, conflict and communication styles, and overall demeanor toward customer service.

Here are some suggested interview questions:

1. Describe a time when you had to deal with a difficult customer (or fellow student, teammate, etc.). How did you work with this person, and what was the outcome?
2. Describe a time when you disagreed with a co-worker (or teammate, family member, etc.) and what you did to resolve the disagreement. How did it turn out?
3. Share with me your personal customer service philosophy. How do you intend to live it if you work for us?
4. Give me an example of when you went the extra mile to satisfy a customer. What did you do?

5. Tell me about a time when you chose to set aside a company policy to meet a customer's needs. How did it turn out?

6. Please read our mission statement and tell me in your own words what it means to you and how you will personally apply it on the job if we hire you.

Note that these kinds of behavior-based questions leave no room for simple "yes or no" answers. They will give a better feel for how a candidate will perform under pressure by giving insights into their personality and values. Remember, "an ounce of prevention is better than a pound of cure." Any leader who has had to go through the process of firing an employee knows this is true.

Number Five: The Power of Treating Folks Right

Here is the reality: internal customers (staff) will rarely treat external customers better than they are being treated by the company (or by each other).

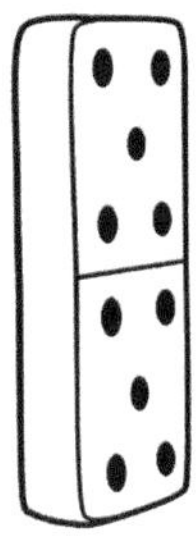

I once watched a store manager belittle and berate a down-cast young employee for leaving some part of his job undone. The outright cruelty, the abuse of positional power, literally poisoned the air in the room. When I went up to the employee a few minutes later to be served, the "glazed eye" look, the sullen resentment, was still radiant. I saw other customers who felt it as well. What a tragic and tremendous cost to this company! I decided then not to do business again with that store.

As a leader, fiercely protect employees from your own weaknesses and their fellow employees' weaknesses. Some ideas include:

1. Insist on, and personally model, that all people are treated with respect, dignity, and courtesy.

2. Nip back-biting, belittling, and insulting behaviors in the bud, instantly and sometimes publicly, to show that such things are non-negotiable.

3. At the same time, reward instances when you see employees and managers treating each other well.

4. Publish a Team Member Bill of Rights and see that it is always enforced. Some examples may be the right to be respected,

the right to try and fail, and the right to state your opinion and be valued for doing so.

5. With everyone's input, create a Code of Conduct that defines how team members treat each other and the customer. The code could include principles such as "we don't gossip or repeat gossip," "we come to work on time and ready to work," and "we start and end meetings on time." When someone forgets or violates a rule, a simple reminder to "stick to the code" will often do the trick.

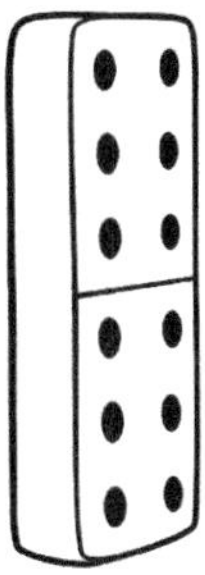

Number Six: The Power of Building Service Teams

Daniel Webster said, *"Men can do jointly what they cannot do singly and the union of hearts and minds, the concentration of power, becomes almost omnipotent."*

Great leaders learn to synergize individuals' unique strengths into powerful teams, which is critical in building a service organization. Quite often, we tend to create what I call "functional silos" in our organization: the cashier silo, the stock silo, the meat-department silo, the management silo. People work in their silos, oblivious and uncaring about the work done in other silos. This generates the "not my job syndrome," the "go ask that guy over there" syndrome, and the "someone should take care of that customer" syndrome, all of which sicken any service system.

Work groups consist of individuals assigned to occupy a similar time and place. Teams are an energetic group of people who are committed to achieving common objectives, who work well together and enjoy doing so, and who produce high-quality results in a united effort. Work groups simply happen, and teams are consciously, deliberately, and constantly built.

The smallest details can rule in customer service. A customer can have great service throughout the store and be treated rudely by the cashier, and all may be lost. Some research shows it takes as many as twelve positive experiences to overcome one extremely negative one, even if there is a chance to recover from it. So, great service is delivered by teams who can cross-function for each other and know enough about each other's work to serve in at least the basic ways.

"Customer service is not a department, it's everyone's job." —Anonymous

1. Promote feelings of achievement and contribution by recognizing the value of the team's work and focusing them on the mission. The ABC rule is achievement, belongingness, and contribution.

2. Promote feelings of belongingness in the team. Encourage the creation of warm connections among team members.

3. Create opportunities for individuals and teams to feel the joy of making real contributions.

4. De-emphasize positions, power, and hierarchies. Create self-directed work teams, but don't fall into the rut of some leaders who carry this too far and abandon their teams.

5. Celebrate team accomplishments, not just individual achievements. Remember, you get what you reward, so if you want teamwork, reward teamwork! A friend of mine who manages a fast-food restaurant promised his employees that if they could, as a team, have perfect closings for thirty days running, he would rent a theater for a midnight showing of the newly released Star Wars movie. His workers were so fired up that they came to work even when they were not scheduled, late at night, to be sure things were perfect. He then traded the midnight showing with the theater manager for a catered party for the theater employees. Clever!

6. Engage in frequent team-building activities. Hint: *The Encyclopedia of Team-building Activities*, published by Jossey-Bass, is a great source, and there are others. Remember, great teams do not just happen. They are consciously built.

7. When possible, assign projects to be done by teams rather than individuals, and challenge the team to beat a previous record or other marks on the wall.

8. Use a code of conduct described previously to govern and moderate team and individual behavior.

"Everyone in an organization should be involved with customer service, not only are they feeling the customer but they are getting a feeling for what's not working."
—Penny Handscomb, British talent and leadership coach

Number Seven: The Power of Challenging Your Processes

The final force multiplier is very crucial. Leaders know that nothing is ever perfect and that all systems can be improved. This does not mean to engage in change for change's sake. People resist "flavor of the month" initiatives. It does mean that we are constantly benchmarking ourselves and stretching to find new and better ways to do business and serve customers.

This has become increasingly critical in recent years. It is now almost impossible to rely on products or price differentiation alone to carve a niche in the market. As soon as a good idea or product is released, competitors mirror it.

The way to truly differentiate is first having the right people, then top-notch service policies, procedures, and strategies. To do this, challenge every process, every procedure, and every policy to see if there is a better way to do it *from the customer's standpoint.*

Most organizations tend over time to organize and create procedures and policies that make work easier or more efficient from the employees' standpoint, not the customer's. As mentioned previously, managers also tend to write policies to cover every unusual situation, not recognizing that they have created an extra step or frustration for 99% of their employees. Soon, policy and procedures manuals are inches thick, and customer frustrations a mile high. Some organizations and leaders punish the 99 for the mistakes of the one, meaning when one staff member does something amiss, they create a policy that constrains and punishes everyone.

A great religious leader was asked over a century ago how he successfully governed a disparate group of converts from a dozen nations. He simply said, "I teach them correct principles, and they govern themselves." We can follow this creed in our own leadership at home and at work. Challenge the process, reduce as much as possible into clear principles, and release employees to govern themselves accordingly.

To challenge the process successfully, I suggest the following:

- Constantly examine the operation as a customer. Call in as a phone customer: what is the phone system like? Start in the parking lot and examine every minute point of impact where a customer engages the services. What is frustrating? What looks good? When there is something wrong, fix it!
- Reward problem-*solving* not problem-*finding*. Challenge others to not bring a problem without at least two possible solutions and a recommendation of which one is best. If you reward problem-finding there may soon be a pack of golden retrievers happily bringing more problems to solve. Send them back for solutions!
- Engage in frequent brainstorming sessions to uncover and solve sticky problems. I recommend posting a challenge of the week for employees to mull over from Monday to Friday, then having a fast-moving brainstorming session to find solutions.
- Shop the competition and do research to benchmark what the very best are doing. Never get complacent.

My last example and story is from the Ritz Carlton hotel chain, which has repeatedly won honors as the top luxury class leader in its field. It created a vision or slogan for all employees: *"We are ladies and gentlemen serving ladies and gentlemen."*

A friend related a situation he witnessed in a Ritz Carlton Hotel. A woman was struggling with her luggage at the door because no bellhop was present. A maintenance man was high on a ladder, replacing a light bulb in the ceiling. He witnessed the situation, climbed down from his ladder, and carried the woman's luggage through check-in, onto the elevator, and to her room.

My friend was so impressed he approached the man and asked him why he did it, and the man simply repeated the Ritz Carlton slogan: "I'm a gentleman, serving a lady," and returned to his work on the ladder.

There was no silo there, only a team member's commitment to satisfy the customer.

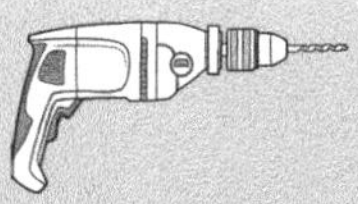

Personal Application Ideas

Bring your teams together to brainstorm ideas on how to create a superb service team. Create action teams to carry out some of the ideas.

Create a library of great customer service books, such as those in the book list in the next Toolbox. Hold book discussions and perhaps assign staff members to lead the discussions.

Watch my video clips on customer loyalty on www.VisionBound.com, or on the Vision Bound YouTube channel.

TOOL NUMBER NINE

My Best of the Best Book List

1. *The Leadership Challenge* by Barry Kouzes and James M. Posner
2. *Drive* by Daniel Pink
3. *If it Ain't Broke... Break it!* by Robert Kriegel
4. *Leading Change* by John P. Kotter
5. *Customers Only Want Two Things: Winning Loyalty in a Competitive World* by Kevin R. Miller
6. *Start with Why* by Simon Sinek
7. E*xtreme Ownership: How U.S. Navy SEALs Lead and Win* by Jocko Willink and Leif Babin
8. *The Speed of Trust* by Stephen M. R. Covey
9. *Blue Ocean Strategy* by W. Chan Kim
10. *Influencer* by Joseph Grenny, Kerry Patterson, David Maxfield, Ron McMillan, and Al Switzler
11. *It's Your Ship* by Captain Michael Abrashoff
12. *The Seven Habits of Highly Effective People* and *The Seven Habits of Highly Effective Families* by Stephen R. Covey
13. *The 4 Disciplines of Execution* by Chris McChesney, Sean Covey, and Jim Huling
14. *The Five Dysfunctions of a Team* by Patrick Lencione
15. *Trap Tales: Outsmarting the Seven Hidden Obstacles to Success* by David M. R. Covey and Stephan M. Mardyks
16. *Crucial Conversations: Tools for Talking When the Stakes are High and Crucial Accountability* by Kerry Patterson, Joseph Grenny,

Ron McMillan, and Al Switzler

17. *Good to Great and Built to Last* by Jim Collins
18. *Talent is Overrated* by Geoff Colvin
19. *Culture Eats Strategy for Lunch* by Curt Coffman and Kathie Sorensen
20. *First Break all the Rules* by Marcus Buckingham
21. *Sticking Points* by Haydn Shaw
22. *Leaders: The Strategies for Taking Charge* by Warren Bennis and Burt Nanus
23. *It's Okay to Manage Your Boss* by Bruce Tulgan
24. *Emotional Intelligence and Working Emotional Intelligence* by Daniel Goleman
25. *1001 Ways to Reward Employees and 1001 Ways to Energize Employees* by Bob Nelson
26. *The Game of Work* by Charles Coonradt
27. *Customer Satisfaction is Worthless: Customer Loyalty is Priceless* by Jeffrey Gittomer
28. *Real World Customer Service Strategies that Really Work* by Kevin R. Miller and other authors
29. *Delivering Knock Your Socks Off Service* by Kristin L. Anderson and Ron Zemke
30. *A Complaint is a Gift* by Janelle Barlow
31. *Customers as Partners* by Chip Bell
32. *Why We Buy* by Paco Underhill
33. *Entrepreneur on Fire* by Kevin R. Miller and other authors
34. *Built to Last* by James Collins and Jerry Porras
35. *The Boys in the Boat* by David James Brown
36. *The Talent Code* by Daniel Coyle
37. *Peak* by Anders Ericsson and Robert Pool
38. *Daring Greatly* by Brene Brown
39. *The Love Prescription: Seven Days to More Intimacy, Connection, and Joy* by John and Julie Gottman
40. *The Law of Love* by Steve Young
41. *Customer Love* by Chip Bell
42. *What Motivates Me* by Adrian Gostick
43. *The Game of Work: How to Enjoy Work as Much as Play* by Charles Coonradt

TOOL NUMBER TEN

Great Quotes Aligned with the Helm Model

"Only three things happen naturally in organizations: friction, confusion, and underperformance. Everything else requires leadership."

—Peter Drucker

"Being in power is like being a lady: if you have to tell people you are, you aren't!"

—Lady Margaret Thatcher, former prime minister of England

"The task of leadership is not to create greatness in people, but to elicit it, for the greatness is already there."

—John Buchan

"There is a difference between leadership and management. Leadership is of the spirit, compounded of personality, vision, and training. Its practice is an art. Management is a science of the mind. Managers are necessary; leaders are indispensable."

—Admiral Thomas Moorer

"Failing organizations are usually over-managed and under-led."

—Warren G. Bennis

"The most pathetic person in the world is someone who has sight but has no vision."

—Helen Keller

"Leadership is communicating to other people their worth and potential so clearly that they come to see it in themselves."

—Stephen R. Covey

"The highest destiny of individuals is to serve rather than to rule."

—Albert Einstein

"I teach them correct principles and let them govern themselves."

—Joseph Smith, religious leader

"Perpetual optimism is a force multiplier."

—General Collin Powell

"Leadership is the capacity to translate vision into reality."

—Warren G. Bennis

"When a thing is done, its done. Don't look back. Look forward to your next objective."

—General George C. Marshall

"The deepest principle in human nature is the craving to be appreciated."

—William James

"People may not remember what you said, but they will always remember how you made them feel."

—Mother Theresa, Carol Buchner, and others

"Catch people in the act of doing something right."

—Ken Blanchard.

"The size of a leader is determined by the depth of his convictions, the height of his ambitions, the breadth of his vision and the reach of his love."

—D. N. Jackson

"A less than perfect decision, made in a timely manner, and vigorously executed, is better than the best decision made too late."

—General George S. Patton

"You can buy people's time; you can buy their physical presence at a given place; you can even buy a measured number of their muscular motions per hour. But you cannot buy enthusiasm, you cannot buy loyalty, you cannot buy the devotion of their hearts. You must earn these."

—Clarence Francis

"The vision of an organization acts as its magnetic north. It possesses the extraordinary ability to attract human energy. It invites and draws others to it by the force of its own appeal."

—Barry Posner and James M. Kouzes

"Brains, like hearts, go where they are appreciated."

—Robert McNamara, Former U.S. Secretary of Defense

"People want to learn new things, to feel they've made a contribution—that what they are doing is worthwhile work. Few people are motivated only by money. People want to feel that what they do makes a difference in the world."

—Frances Hesselbein, president of the Peter F. Drucker Foundation

"Outstanding leaders go out of their way to boost the self-esteem of their personnel. If people believe in themselves, it's amazing what they can accomplish."

—Sam Walton, founder of Walmart

"Never tell people how to do things. Tell them what to do and they will surprise you with their ingenuity."

—General George S. Patton

"Again and again, the impossible problem is solved when we see that the problem is only a tough decision waiting to be made."

—Robert Schuller

"Do what you can with what you have where you are."

—Teddy Roosevelt

"Little value comes out of the belief that people will respond progressively better by treating them progressively worse."

—Eric Harvey

"No executive has ever suffered because his subordinates were strong and effective."

—Peter Drucker

"A common theme present in most discussions of leadership for the 21st century is the leader's ability to create, articulate, and communicate not only a vision but, more importantly, a global vision."

—Karin Klenke

"Greatness lies not in being strong, but in the right use of strength."

—Henry Ward Beecher

"Avoid having your ego so close to your position that when your position falls, your ego goes with it."

—Colin Powell

"If you aren't making any mistakes, it's a sure sign you're playing it too safe."

—John Maxwell

"A leader is a dealer in hope."

—Napoleon Bonaparte

"If you cannot do great things, do small things in a great way."

—Napoleon Bonaparte

"No man is fit to command another that cannot command himself."

—William Penn

"A man who wants to lead the orchestra must turn his back on the crowd."

—James Cook

"It often happens that I wake at night and begin to think about a serious problem and decide I must tell the Pope about it. Then I wake up completely and remember that I am the Pope."

—Pope John XXIII

"My definition of a leader...is a man who can persuade people to do what they don't want to do, or do what they're too lazy to do, and like it."

—Harry S. Truman

"Leadership: the art of getting someone else to do something you want done because he wants to do it."

—Dwight D. Eisenhower

"Trust becomes a verb when you communicate to others their worth and potential so clearly that they are inspired to see it in themselves."

—Stephen Covey

"Complaining is misery's mating call."

— Lauren McDonald

"I don't know what I said until you tell me what you heard."

— Major General Douglas Crissman

VISIONBOUND™
International

The VisionBound Story

The Loyalty Company

I founded VisionBound International in 1996 when I retired from my service as an active duty U.S. Army officer. In that role, I became passionate about the power of great leadership, having seen the effects of great and poor leadership in Army units.

The mission of VisionBound is "to accelerate greatness by releasing human potential" because we believe in the great innate potential that lies in all human beings. It is tragic that over half of employed people feel no job satisfaction and most are only giving the minimum effort needed to emotionally and mentally survive at work. We want to turn this around by bringing light and hope. However, the old saying is true, "Hope is NOT a strategy." We must provide people, leaders and teams with the skills, tools, energy and passion needed to make sustainable change.

In the past twenty years, we have worked to bring under one umbrella dozens of courses and workshops. We think of these as "Lego bricks" which can be assembled into whatever combination you need, based on our free team assessments. Our Vital Signs survey is a free offer we use to help "diagnose before we prescribe."

We typically explain our approach with the "Three Lane Model." You'll move forward along three lanes, which are linked together: **Win Loyal Customers, Provide Inspiring Leadership** and **Build Winning Teams.** Programs in each of these lanes allow you to start anywhere in the model.

We prefer to start in the **Win Loyal Customers** lane with our flagship program *Customers Only Want Two Things: Winning Loyal Customers*. The program teaches winning loyalty both inside and outside the company with a refreshing new approach. A companion workshop provides managers with ideas and skills on how to build and empower a service team, and a third workshop addresses how to work with difficult customers.

This series couples nicely with our extensive array of customizable leadership academies within our **VisionBound Leadership Institute**. We have learned that nothing is sustainable without great leadership.

Along the way, we can assist you in the third lane of **Building Winning Teams** with half- to full-day team-building retreats and workshops. These are packed with great team-building activities teaching healthy communication, uniting employees around a common team purpose, and creating a team Code of Conduct to govern behaviors.

We have learned that all of this does not work well when a company does not follow their **North Star** with a clearly defined vision, mission, values, strategy, and goals. Studies show that only about 15% of people know their company's North Star and it is often unclear and fuzzy even at the executive level. VisionBound offers a fine program of strategic planning, usually off-site with executive and senior leaders, to guide them in creating this clear North Star.

For all these reasons, we brand ourselves *"The Loyalty Company"* because our goal is to create a culture of loyalty. We want to help companies and teams take themselves to new levels of focus and achievement and create a culture that will win loyalty among all their stakeholders. We can all work together to release the human potential in your company.

How We Can Help

1. Experience our full VisionBound *Customers Only Want Two Things: Winning Loyal Customers* program. Each staff member will receive the Hot Tip Deck, many QuickCards and other tools to win loyalty. Our *Building and Leading a Service Team* seminar instills managers with skills to create a service culture.

2. Our *VisionBound Leadership Institute* will instill inspiring leadership throughout your organization, from executives to your next-generation of emerging leaders.

3. Participate in our no-cost offer: a Vital Signs Survey that will gauge the level of loyalty in your staff and measure over thirty indicators of a successful company. See a sample at www.surveymonkey.com/r/vssample.

4. Be sure to watch our video clips on our website or on the VisionBound YouTube channel.

5. Benefit from our other customized assessment and survey tools, including our Strength-Based Leader 360 Profile.

6. VisionBound at Sea: we will take your team on an amazing learning adventure aboard a cruise ship somewhere in the world, combining learning with relaxation, team building and fun. See www.visionboundatsea.com.

7. We are available for a wide variety of other services, from strategic planning sessions to keynote addresses and break-out sessions.

Contact Information

VisionBound International, LLC: www.visionbound.com, info@visionbound.com

To reach the author directly: Kevin@visionbound.com

Testimonials for the Program

"We invited Kevin to bring his outstanding leadership program to over 100 bank managers from rural banks in Ghana, Africa. The response was overwhelmingly positive, and they all resonated with the power of the Helm Model and how Kevin oriented the concepts. We are now poised to start offering this program, and his customer loyalty program, across the continent of Africa. I promise if you bring this program to your team, you will see very positive results from their new vision, energy, and tools."

—Mike Osikoya, CEO of Mikensy Consulting in Ghana

"We brought Kevin in several times to work with all our leaders from within the U.S. and Brazil. The powerful tools he presented have helped focus and unite all our managers to a renewed vision, mission, and strategy he helped us create. He has a very innovative way to unite people in thinking about and focusing on goals, both strategic and operational. As CEO, I have seen very positive outcomes from his inspired teaching and consulting."

—Ray Fuchs, President of EcoBrite Solutions and RFF Enterprises

About the Author

Kevin R. Miller is founder and CEO of VisionBound International LLC, and VisionBound at Sea, and founder of VisionBound Africa. He served as an active duty U.S. Army Officer, including as a company commander in the 7th Infantry Division. He is passionate about unleashing the potential of people, teams and organizations. He has had the unique opportunity to work with a wide range of companies, from Fortune 100 companies to small entrepreneurial companies, as well as government, military, education and state and civic organizations. Kevin holds graduate degrees from Kansas State University and Utah State University and is a graduate of the U.S. Army Command and General Staff College, where he also served as an instructor. He has taught at three universities. Kevin lives with his wife, Denise, in Springville, Utah. They have four children and six grandchildren.

About the Illustrator

Izabela Ciesinka was born in Poland and grew up in Toronto, Canada. She has illustrated for clients like Oxford University Press, Sunshine Books, the Pentecostal Publishing House, and the Concordia Publishing House, for whom she illustrated the picture book *Prayer: Learning How to Talk to God.* Izabela has also created artwork for game companies, as well as character designs for animation projects. In February 2024, she had her author's debut with the picture book *The Little Donkey and God's Big Plan* (Ascension Press), which she also illustrated.

In her spare time, she likes reading good books, discovering great cinema, taking (very) long walks, and watching cute animal videos on YouTube.

Contact Izzi at izzipop2003@yahoo.com.

About the Editor

Abigail Ellis is an editor from Kaysville, Utah. She graduated from Brigham Young University in December 2023 with a bachelors in Editing and Publishing and a minor in Business. Although new to the career field, Abigail isn't new to editing. While in school, she was editor in chief of *Schwa: Language and Linguistics*, a semesterly journal focused on student linguistic research, and the managing editor for two online blogs, *Latter-day Saint Insights* and *Editing Research.*

Stories are a big part of Abigail's life. On any given day, you can find her watching a movie, reading a book, or retelling a favorite story to someone else.

Contact Abby at abbyfellis@gmail.com.